Inspirational and to-the-point. If you wa[nt]
worked through those early Methodists t[o]
tion movement, then read this book! Bevins calls us to learn from the
wisdom of those who have gone before us, and we must heed his call.
Read, learn, and apply!

J. D. PAYNE, PROFESSOR OF CHRISTIAN MINISTRY AT SAMFORD
UNIVERSITY AND AUTHOR OF *APOSTOLIC CHURCH PLANTING*

With a powerful simplicity, Bevins has written a brief book distill-
ing John Wesley's wisdom of the past to help us move forward on
God's mission. His excellent overview of Wesley's life and strategies of
"movement making" are crystal clear and compelling. For any leader
interested in seeing a gospel movement, *Marks of a Movement* is an
essential resource.

REV. DR. LARRY WALKEMEYER, LEAD PASTOR, LIGHT & LIFE
CHRISTIAN FELLOWSHIP; SUPERINTENDENT, SOUTHERN CALIFORNIA
FREE METHODIST; DIRECTOR OF EQUIPPING, EXPONENTIAL

History at its best accurately reflects on what happened and builds
vision for what can yet happen. Bevins highlights the people and the
practices of one of the great movements of Christianity—and inspires
us to multiply disciples and churches in our generation.

WAYNE SCHMIDT, GENERAL SUPERINTENDENT, THE WESLEYAN CHURCH

Winfield masterfully summarizes John Wesley and the Methodist
movement. If you want to see a church multiplication movement happen in your context today, this is required reading.

DANIEL IM, AUTHOR OF *NO SILVER BULLETS*, COAUTHOR
OF *PLANTING MISSIONAL CHURCHES*, AND DIRECTOR OF
CHURCH MULTIPLICATION, NEWCHURCHES.COM

Marks of a Movement is a concise account of the characteristics of the
Methodist movement and its application for today. I've read a lot of
material on John Wesley and the Methodists, but this book has some

valuable surprises. Don't miss this opportunity to learn from one of the greatest movements in history.

STEVE ADDISON, AUTHOR OF *PIONEERING MOVEMENTS*

It's impossible to read this book without getting excited about what the Holy Spirit has done and can do in lives fully surrendered to God. This account of the powerful marks of the Wesleyan movement inspires and challenges us to be part of the birth of a new movement for our day. On almost every page I found myself praying: "May it happen again!"

REV. JESSICA LaGRONE, DEAN OF THE CHAPEL, ASBURY SEMINARY

The method of John Wesley created the greatest religious movement in American history. Could it hold the key to the next great movement in US history? Bevins thinks so. Drawing from the life and ministry of John Wesley, Bevins describes key marks of a movement. Anyone interested in joining the growing multiplication movement should read this book.

BILL EASUM, PRESIDENT, THE EFFECTIVE CHURCH GROUP

"A brand plucked from the burning"—my countryman John Wesley started a fiery movement of reproducing disciples, leaders, and churches that reflected the purity, simplicity, and communal power of the early church. His followers took the apostolic church of Acts as their model and set their world on fire with passion. It's vital to learn again from the man and his ministry, but most of all from his methods. I am thrilled that Dr. Bevins helps us do so here, and in such a readable manner.

ANTHONY DELANEY, LEADER FOR THE IVY NETWORK,
NEWTHING UK AND LAUNCH CONFERENCE

Winfield Bevins reminds us of John Wesley's disciple-making wisdom, which gave birth to a movement of mission and church planting. The movement he started spread around the world and ultimately transformed the religious landscape of the West. With his love for the history of the church and his personal experience of church planting, Bevins helps us understand powerful lessons from John Wesley that can inspire hero makers today.

CHRISTIAN SELVARATNAM, HEAD OF CHURCH PLANTING ENGAGEMENT, ALPHA UK & EUROPE; LEADER OF G2 YORK

Marks of a Movement is a handful of gems for the movement-maker—giving them precious and short reflections on some of our most brilliant forbearers in church revival. Winfield Bevins is a unique voice bringing together mainline leaders, church planters, and dreamers from across a huge spectrum. I have great faith for what this guide can bring!

GRAHAM SINGH, EXECUTIVE DIRECTOR OF CHURCH PLANTING CANADA AND RECTOR OF ST. JAX MONTREAL

The twenty-first century demands a new and revitalized apostolic movement of disciple-making leaders like never before in the history of the church. This book will become a blueprint to accomplish such a monumental task for those seeking to establish the kingdom of God.

REV DR. IOSMAR ALVAREZ, SENIOR PASTOR OF FUENTE DE AVIVAMIENTO AND FOUNDER OF DISCIPLE 21 NETWORK

To re-evangelize the postmodern West, it will take not just a method or program, but a movement. Taking his cues from the early Wesleyan movement, Winfield Bevins offers clear and wise guidance on how we might reignite the fire that once spread so rapidly across England and the nascent United States, and eventually, throughout the globe. I strongly recommend this book for all those with a heart to win the lost and see revival in the increasingly secular context of the postmodern West.

DAVID F. WATSON, PHD, ACADEMIC DEAN, VICE PRESIDENT FOR ACADEMIC AFFAIRS, AND PROFESSOR OF NEW TESTAMENT AT UNITED THEOLOGICAL SEMINARY

When God breathes his Spirit upon his followers for his purpose, movements are birthed. While these movements of God are easy to spot, they can be difficult to understand. In *Marks of a Movement*, Winfield Bevins helps us do exactly that. Drawing from a deep well of tried-and-true practices, he reframes old paradigms for a modern audience. You will finish this book with a fresh understanding of past movements of God and a burning passion to see God to do the same again today.

ROBBY GALLATY, PASTOR, LONG HOLLOW BAPTIST AND
AUTHOR, *GROWING UP* AND *HERE AND NOW*

Two hundred years ago, Methodism was the greatest soul-winning discipleship movement in America. If you want to know how the church can recover its mission and live again, Winfield Bevins tells how!"

DR. ROBERT COLEMAN, AUTHOR OF *THE MASTER PLAN OF EVANGELISM*

Jesus said a person well-trained for the kingdom of God is "like the master of a household who brings out of his treasure things old and new" (Matt.13:52). A key truth for church renewal: linking the old and new. John Wesley understood this and modeled it better perhaps than anyone else in history. The dynamics, depth, and discipleship of early Methodism grew from the combustive joining of the Great Tradition with the newness of the Spirit in people's lives. *Marks of a Movement* brings these old/new insights into our present time. Today, Jesus can and will renew persons, churches, even whole societies, and here early Methodism and other movements can teach us. Churches today often struggle along with only half their true DNA. *Marks of a Movement* shows why, and what to do. Here is new wine enriched by the old of past movements."

HOWARD A. SNYDER, AUTHOR OF *THE RADICAL WESLEY*, *THE PROBLEM OF WINESKINS*, AND *SIGNS OF THE SPIRIT*, AND INTERNATIONAL REPRESENTATIVE, MANCHESTER WESLEY RESEARCH CENTRE

Marks of a Movement is well worth reading to the very, very end! It is a very practical book that shows how John Wesley innovated, and how we should do the same, if we want a multiplying movement like his in our day.

MICHAEL MOYNAGH, AUTHOR OF *CHURCH IN LIFE: INNOVATION, MISSION AND ECCLESIOLOGY* AND TUTOR, WYCLIFFE HALL, OXFORD

Scott Adams, creator of Dilbert, once devised a Mission Statement Generator, which could be loaded with familiar buzzwords to automatically formulate high-toned bunk. Winfield Bevins has done the opposite—written a Mission Detector book that finds and refines those core missional components that make and mark an authentic movement of the Spirit in every age and context. Regardless of tribe, this book is required reading for all feeling called to participate in God's missional renaissance.

LEONARD SWEET, AUTHOR OF *BAD HABITS OF JESUS*, PROFESSOR AT DREW UNIVERSITY, GEORGE FOX UNIVERSITY, TABOR COLLEGE, EVANGELICAL SEMINARY, AND FOUNDER OF PREACHTHESTORY.COM

MARKS OF A MOVEMENT

ALSO BY WINFIELD BEVINS

Ever Ancient, Ever New

MARKS OF A MOVEMENT

What the Church Today Can Learn

from the Wesleyan Revival

WINFIELD BEVINS

ZONDERVAN
REFLECTIVE

ZONDERVAN REFLECTIVE

Marks of a Movement
Copyright © 2019 by Winfield Bevins

Requests for information should be addressed to:
Zondervan, *3900 Sparks Dr. SE, Grand Rapids, Michigan 49546*

ISBN 978-0-310-09835-5 (softcover)

ISBN 978-0-310-09325-1 (ebook)

Art direction: Darren Welch Design
Cover Photos: ChrisBellPhoto / Lightstock.com; whitemay / iStockphoto.com
Interior design: Denise Froelich

Printed in the United States of America

19 20 21 22 23 /LSC/ 10 9 8 7 6 5 4 3 2 1

To
Timothy Tennent, Tom Tumlin, and Howard Snyder
Scholars, Mentors, and Friends

CONTENTS

FOREWORD

Many readers will find Winfield Bevins' new book an engaging, instructive, and inspiring read, and one of the most notable books on church multiplication written in this century. The book draws substantially from the strategic wisdom of John Wesley. Bevins is not a Methodist, but he is yet another non-Methodist thinker who perceives stashes of gold in Methodism's lore that most Methodists now ignore.

Not that this is a book only, or even primarily, for Methodists. It draws important insights from other traditions, such as Moravians, Baptists, Pentecostals, and Anglicans, and from case studies historical, current, and global. And in its application, the book is relevant to every Christian tradition.

Donald McGavran used to talk about the strategic importance of "the multiplication of units" to Christian movements. Bevins gets this. In his paradigm, church multiplication is intrinsically about multiplying small groups, large groups, congregations, campuses, ministries, and especially leaders . . . and extra-especially Christian disciples.

I am aware that most church leaders have a limited book budget, and that too many books on church multiplication are astonishingly derivative—repeating or restating what has been written before, almost to the point of serial plagiarism. While *Marks of a Movement* draws from many sources (it refers the reader to a range of good sources), the reader will find a range of significant new insights. For instance, Bevins' discussions of "discipleship systems," and "the stickiness factor," and "the leadership pipeline" will be informing entrepreneurial church leaders many years from now.

Bevins also revisits and reframes some classic themes in ways that help the reader to rediscover their indispensable relevance. I am thinking especially of his reflections on the role of the Holy Spirit in church multiplication.

Can you tell that I like this book? More important, I commend *Marks of a Movement* to all church leaders who want their churches to be less like stagnant institutions and more like contagious movements.

George G. Hunter III
Distinguished Professor Emeritus
Asbury Theological Seminary

INTRODUCTION

Once upon a time, in John Wesley's lifetime
and for another century or more, Methodism
in Great Britain and in North America was a
contagious Christian movement.

GEORGE HUNTER III

I've traveled around the world, but England is by far one of my
favorite countries to visit. Everywhere you step, you uncover
living reminders of our ongoing connection to the past. From
first-century Roman roads to ancient cathedrals, England is
a stunning convergence of old and new. Over the centuries,
it has given the world many great things such as the works of
Shakespeare and Dickens. And although it is little known to
many contemporary Christians, England also gave us one of the
world's great Christian movements: the Wesleyan revival.

On a recent trip to England, I visited several of the historic sites of this revival with a friend. One of the places we

visited was City Road Chapel in London, founded in 1778 by John Wesley. We toured the chapel and walked around Wesley's home. Later, we paused and prayed at Wesley's tomb. Standing there, I was inspired to read these words on his tombstone, an apt description of his enduring legacy:

> To the memory of the venerable John Wesley, A.M., late fellow of Lincoln College, Oxford. This great light arose (by the singular providence of God) to enlighten these nations, and to revive, enforce, and defend, the pure apostolic doctrines and practices of the primitive church: which he continued to do, both by his writings and his labours for more than half a century: And to his inexpressible joy, not only, beheld their influence extending, and their efficacy witness'd in the hearts and lives of many thousands, as well in the western world as in these kingdoms: But also, far above all human power of expectation, liv'd to see provision made by the singular grace of God, for their continuance and establishment to the joy of future generations. Reader, if thou art constrain'd to bless the instrument, give God the glory.

These words remind us that once upon a time, a man named John Wesley helped start a movement that led to the cultural transformation of the English nation, a movement that eventually spread around the world. But how? And why? What made this man and this movement unique? Why did the teachings of Wesley and his practices ignite a wildfire, while other movements began and fizzled out?

Perhaps there is something in what Wesley learned and what he did that we can learn from today. In fact, let me go one step further. Scholars and church historians know the significance of the story of the Wesleyan revival; however, I have discovered that very few people outside Methodism know anything about this movement and its potential impact for the church today. I believe that the life and ministry of John Wesley has something we desperately need. And that's why I've written this book.

John Wesley and Eighteenth Century England

Wesley was born in 1703 and lived for almost 90 years during one of the great paradigm shifting periods of history, what historians refer to as the Age of Reason and the rise of the industrial revolution. The eighteenth century ushered in an era of major cultural change and upheaval. As a result, England was teetering on the verge of anarchy and chaos. This contributed to increased poverty, pollution, and child labor in factories where children as young as six years old worked long hours for little or no pay. As towns and cities grew rapidly around factories, problems such as urban crime, alcohol abuse, gambling, prostitution, and high infant mortality increased. These were dark times for the country, and the future was not all that encouraging. All of this led to a national concern about the spiritual and moral welfare of England and its future.

In 1738, Bishop Berkeley declared that religion and morality in Britain had collapsed "to a degree that was never before known in any Christian country."[1] The Church of England of the eighteenth century was not prepared to deal with the national crisis, and in fact, may have contributed to the overall moral decay. There was an epidemic of spiritual laxity and even widespread immorality among some of the clergy. Many ordained ministers did not have a living faith and sometimes caused more harm than good. This resulted in the Church of England experiencing a rapid decline in church attendance.

In the midst of all this, God led a man named John Wesley to rediscover something lost, reigniting a movement dynamic to the Christian faith that would be felt around the world. Some historians have suggested that the Wesleyan revival saved England from a bloody revolution like the one France would shortly experience.[2] John Wesley sought to recover a basic understanding of what it means to be a real Christian. His original vision was to bring spiritual renewal to the Church of England, which was not well received. Yet despite the growing tension between Wesley and the institutional church, we should not forget that both he and his brother, Charles, were ordained in the Church of England.

It's easy to think that Wesley opposed church tradition altogether. Nothing could be farther from the truth. In fact, he was a high churchman who loved the Anglican liturgy. He used the Church of England's *Book of Common Prayer*, which contains orders of services, ancient creeds, communal prayers, and a lectionary, which is a suggested reading plan for use throughout the liturgical year. Wesley said, "I believe there is no Liturgy in the world, either in ancient or modern language, which breathes more of a solid, scriptural, rational piety than the Common Prayer of the Church of England."[3] While at Oxford, Wesley and Charles were accused of being "sacramentalists" because of their insistence upon taking communion regularly. It is said that Wesley took the Lord's Supper at least once every four to five days, and he encouraged the Methodists to celebrate the Lord's Supper weekly. Wesley said, "It is the duty of every Christian to receive the Lord's Supper as often as he can."[4] These are hardly the words of a non-traditionalist.

While he wasn't against tradition, Wesley *was* opposed to dead, dry religion, cold ritualism, and the clericalism that discouraged non-ordained people from being involved in the life of the ministry, all of which had become widespread in the Church of England in the eighteenth century.

It was never the intention of the Wesley brothers to separate from the Church of England. They viewed Methodism as a renewal movement *within* the Church. When asked point-blank if he wanted to separate from the Church of England, Wesley affirmed his allegiance: "I am fully convinced that our Church (of England), with all her blemishes, is nearer the scriptural plan than any other in Europe."[5] Later in life, he affirmed this yet again, saying, "I will not separate from the Church; yet, secondly, in case of necessity I will vary from it (both of which I have constantly and openly avowed for upwards of fifty years) and inconsistency vanishes away. I have been true to my profession from 1730 to this day."[6]

While it was Wesley's intention to remain part of the institutional church, the old wineskins of the Church of England could not contain the new wine of the Wesleyan revival. What started off as a spiritual renewal within the Church of England eventually became its own distinct movement, which we will discuss in later chapters. By the time of John Wesley's death in 1791, Methodism was an international church movement with more than seventy thousand members in England and more than forty thousand in the new United States, with even more among the mission stations scattered around the world. The seeds of the Methodist movement would continue to grow and spread well beyond Wesley's lifetime. Just a few years after his death, Methodism in North America had grown to two hundred thousand, with more than four thousand Methodist preachers. By 1830, official membership in the Methodist Church had reached almost half a million people, and attenders numbered six million.[7] From 1880 to 1905, American Methodism planted more than seven hundred churches per year on average.[8]

One of the secrets of the success of Wesley's movement was his willingness to embrace change, his ability to maintain a dynamic synthesis of old and new, tradition and innovation.[9] Rather than resisting the changes looming on the horizon, Wesley's leadership created a contagious movement that proactively engaged the culture, preparing the church to be a force of change in society rather than simply reacting to cultural change. Wesley returned the Christian faith and practice to its roots by emphasizing radical discipleship and vital relationships, and this renewed emphasis transformed the religious landscape of much of the Western world for the next two centuries.

At the heart of the Wesleyan revival was the rediscovery of "the pure apostolic doctrines and practices of the early church." But Wesley did more than read and study the past. He took what he learned and reapplied it, contextualizing it to his own time and place. More than that, he used what he learned to create a disciple-making movement that equipped and empowered thousands of people to join in God's mission.

During his lifetime, Wesley traveled more than 250,000 miles, preached over 40,560 sermons, and led thousands of people to Christ. With skill and discipline, he quickly became one of the most influential leaders of the evangelical awakening of the eighteenth century, a movement that reached thousands of people during his lifetime alone. The Wesleyan revival began with just a handful of people in the early 1700s, quickly growing into a resurgence movement leading to the establishment of thousands of societies in England and in the United States.

About This Book

For the last decade, I've studied historic church movements—how they have succeeded and why they have sometimes failed. I've spent time with church movement thinkers like Steve Addison,

Alan Hirsh, Howard Snyder, and George Hunter III, among others. One of the reasons I have come to believe we need to study movements is the fact that so many churches and denominations in Europe and North America are declining rather than growing, even as the population around them has more than quadrupled in size. Eighty to eighty-five percent of all churches in the United States have either stopped growing or are now in decline, and an estimated three to four thousand churches close their doors each year.[10] It is estimated that 660–700 thousand people are leaving the traditional church every year.[11] The Pew Research Center has found that nearly one third of young adults now say they have no religious affiliation. This young-adult group has been nicknamed the "nones" because they disavow association with any organized form of religion. If we treated them as a group, they would be the second largest religious group in North America.[12] And this is not just an American church problem. In England, church membership has declined from 10.6 million in 1930 to 5.5 Million in 2010; from about 30 percent to 11.2 percent. If current trends continue, membership is forecast to decline to 2.53 million (4.3 percent of the population) by 2025. The avowedly non-religious—similar to the North American "nones"—now make up 48.6 percent of the British population.[13]

I believe the solution to these problems requires more than behavioral research and the latest spin on church growth theory. I would argue that much of contemporary church growth theory hasn't worked all that well for the Western church and may even be leading to its decline. I believe the path forward lies, perhaps surprisingly, in the past. How has God historically brought revival and cultural transformation to his church and society? We must study these movements to learn how they work and then ask ourselves, *What can we learn from movements for today?*

I've come away with the deep conviction that in our present

day and age, if we are going to reach the West again with the gospel of Christ, we need *another* movement of the same proportions as the Wesleyan revival of the eighteenth century. The example of the Wesleyan revival offers us vital and timeless lessons for church renewal and fresh expressions of mission in the twenty-first century.

I am confident that the answers we need for the future of God's church will be found at the intersection of the past and the present. As Leonard Sweet reminds us:

> "Postmodern Pilgrims must strive to keep the past and the present in perpetual conversation so every generation will find a fresh expression of the Gospel that is anchored solidly to the faith that was once delivered."[14]

In my experience, many contemporary Christians have historical amnesia, and there are significant gaps in our understanding of the past, especially the past history of the Christian church. Because of this, we are missing vital aspects of our faith that are necessary for spiritual growth and maturity. This lack of historic awareness, I believe, can be remedied by studying movements like the Wesleyan revival and asking ourselves what these movements can teach us about discipleship and multiplication.

If you are a Christ-follower who is tired of hearing about church decline, and if you are hungry to see a fresh movement of God in the West again, this book is written for you. It's not a biography, nor is it an academic history. Rather, my intention is to offer an introduction to the life, ministry, and movement of John Wesley that is understandable, readable, and applicable to our own questions about disciple-making and church multiplication in the twenty-first century. I will be the first to admit that there are many excellent books and articles about John

Wesley—many of them written by Methodists who have spent a lifetime studying Wesley and his methods. I've written this book in the hope of sharing a few nuggets of wisdom from this rich tradition with those outside the Methodist "inner circle." As I travel and speak, I find few people outside of Methodism who really know this man or grasp his impact on the worldwide Christian church.

With that said, I should also make it clear that I am *not* a Methodist. My own tradition is Anglican, so while I share historic roots with John Wesley (who was himself an Anglican priest) I do not belong to the Methodist religious tradition myself. It doesn't matter if you are a Baptist, Anglican, Pentecostal, or Presbyterian reading this book, because there are vital lessons for *all* Christian believers in the life and ministry of John Wesley. And if your own background happens to be Wesleyan or Methodist and you are not familiar with your own tradition, I hope this book will help you rediscover the apostolic impulse of your own heritage.[15] You will be introduced to some of the other leaders of the Wesleyan movement as well as several modern-day examples of churches and believers that have been directly influenced by Wesley and his methods.

One of the key features of our study is an identification of the key marks that characterized the Methodist movement, but I want to emphasize that this list is neither comprehensive nor authoritative. In identifying these marks, my hope is to provide readers with a summary of interrelated factors that reinforce one another and lead to movement multiplication and growth. Some of these factors are correlated by movements other than the Wesleyan revival, and so I've occasionally supplemented what I've written with the insights of other movement studies. I've also included some snapshots from these other movements and some of their key leaders to help you gain a broader understanding of how God works through movements. Several of these key marks lists are available in the appendix to further your own study and research. Perhaps you will find some additional overlap or notice aspects of similarity with other movements that were not emphasized or addressed in this book.

Before we begin, I also want to offer a word of warning. Don't be tempted to think of this or any other movement as a silver bullet to the problems and challenges of today's church, or that if the church can just return to the golden age, all of its problems will be solved. It can be tempting to engage in hero worship when we are looking for positive lessons in history, but we must never forget that movements are messy. They involve broken people and human relationships, and there is always the reality of human sin. This is only multiplied when movements are growing and multiplying. The very dynamism of early Methodism produced all sorts of splits and divisions within the movement, some of which arose from within. I will share some of the weaknesses of the movement in the final chapter. The story of Methodism reminds us that a perfect God uses imperfect people to accomplish his plans on earth.

Finally, my hope is that reading this book will spark some thought about movements in your own context. To that end, I pray that as you read *Marks of a Movement*, it will lead to a disciple-making movement in your life, your church, your community, and our world. It happened then, and it can happen today. May God do it again!

CHAPTER 1

UNDERSTANDING MOVEMENTS

*Movements are one of the key means by which
God brings renewal and expansion to the
church in its mission.*

STEVE ADDISON

Whether we realize it or not, movements are happening all around us. The world is made up of thousands of social movements of people groups from various nations, races, and socioeconomic backgrounds. Some movements are religious, while others are committed to social, environmental, or philosophical issues. Perhaps the simplest definition of movements is a large group of people who are committed to the same cause.

Movements are all about change; often movements are committed to bringing about major change, causing upheaval at local and national levels. Some movements are good, while others are destructive and evil. Take, for instance, the small African nation of Rwanda. In 1994, Rwanda experienced one of the worst genocides in history. In a period of one hundred days, close to one million ethnic Tutsi and moderate Hutu died at the hands of extremist Hutus. The Rwandan genocide left millions of innocent people orphaned or widowed, many of them young children and the elderly. In the face of such an atrocity, it's difficult to imagine anything good coming about as a result, but there were glimmers of hope in the aftermath of the killings. The government called upon the church to help bring healing and reconciliation between the Tutsi and Hutu, joining hands to eradicate poverty and illiteracy. A movement of hate almost destroyed the nation, but it gave birth to a new movement of love and reconciliation, one that has since helped rebuild it.

Movements are often a reaction to or against something like injustice, institutionalization, or corruption. Another example of the power of reactionary social movements was the American Civil Rights movement in the mid-twentieth-century United States. The movement, led by Martin Luther King, Jr. and others, desired to end racial segregation and discrimination against African Americans. At the age of thirty-five, Martin Luther King, Jr. became the youngest man to receive the Nobel Peace Prize. Dr. King's prophetic words inspired a generation, which resulted in legal and social change that empowered black Americans who had been disenfranchised and persecuted for centuries. At the heart of his message were themes of freedom, equality, justice, and love.

The history of the world is a history of social movements changing civilizations. It has been said that if we fail to understand the past, we are doomed to repeat it. And so, to better understand our history and the dynamics that underlie social movements, this chapter will look at what movements are and how they tend to operate. We will be looking at this question from a Christian perspective in particular, asking how and why certain movements have led to transformation and change.

Characteristics of Movements

While all movements have distinct characteristics, there are some common characteristics they all share. Sociologists L. P. Gerlack and V. H. Hine define a movement as:

> a group of people who are organized for, ideologically moti-
> vated by, and committed to a purpose which implements some
> form of personal or social change; who are actively engaged in
> the recruitment of others; and whose influence is spreading in
> opposition to the established order within which it originated.[1]

This definition helps us see movements from a sociological perspective. First, we see that movements involve *people*. In particular, movements involve groups of people or social networks that seek to bring about social change at various levels and degrees within a society or culture. Movements can take place at the local, national, or international level. Church growth expert George Hunter III has developed a helpful summary of what most effective social movements have in common. He refers to these factors as "movement dynamics":

> ***Shared definitions, message, and objectives:*** A move-
> ment is an organized network of people with a shared
> definition of reality, a shared message, and a shared
> cause with shared objectives.

Long-term commitment: A movement is not confined to a single campaign. The people are committed for as long as it takes.

Possess some level of organization: A movement is distinct from mere trends in that it is at least minimally organized. Compared to institutions, however, movements are organized more from the bottom up than from the top down.

May include multiple movements within it: Within effective movements, multiple organized micro-movements usually flourish. Examples would include the many organizations that share a commitment to peace or the health of creation or the several thousand mission orders within the Roman Catholic Church.

No formal bureaucracy: Movements usually lack anything like the leverage of bureaucratic power within the organization or the society they hope to change.

Indiscriminate evangelism: Effective social movements evangelize all the people they can find who are receptive to the cause. The most important factor in whether the movement's cause will ultimately prevail depends on increasing the ranks of the seriously committed.

Pragmatic approach to programs and activities: Effective social movements continually look for ways to widen their scope and influence and to increase their range of programs and activities, while abandoning programs and activities that are no longer effective.

Member identity: In strong movements, many members root their self-identity, at least partly, in their identification with the movement.

Flexible and open to change: Effective movements are

fairly flexible. They can change as they learn, as they grow, and as the context changes.

Communicate publicly and personally: Effective movements communicate their vision and message in two steps: (1) they communicate their message publicly, in as many ways as possible, and (2) the movement's members then engage people who know about the movement in conversation. [2]

Knowing the factors that underlie different social movements can help us better understand how Christianity spreads within a culture. And although we might utilize theological language and biblical concepts to describe Christian movements, we should also recognize that they have similar, overlapping phenomenon common to all movements, and that there is a great deal we can learn from knowing and studying them.

The Christian Movement

Now that we've looked at some general characteristics of movements, let's ask, *What is unique to social movements within Christianity?* At its core, Christianity is more than an institution (like the Orthodox or Roman Catholic Church); it is a movement. The story of Christianity is the amazing and unlikely story of the rise of a religious and sociological movement. With little money and no modern technology or mass marketing strategy, Christianity grew to become one of the world's major religions. The best estimates suggest over two billion followers of Christ worldwide. And it all started when an obscure Jewish teacher named Jesus invited a few ordinary people to follow him.

Few people today deny that Jesus Christ is one of the most, if not *the* most, significant men who has ever walked the earth. He is one of the most loved and most hated men in all of human history. Wars have been waged in his name, and millions of lives have been lost following him. His life, death, and resurrection inspired a revolutionary movement that began over two thousand years ago in what we today call the Middle East and has spread to people all around the world. His small band of followers became the seedbed for the greatest movement the world has ever known.

Jesus' short earthly ministry began when he was thirty years old, and it abruptly ended three years later. Thousands of people followed Jesus to hear his teachings and to witness the miracles he performed. He often spoke in parables—stories with symbolic meaning—to explain deep spiritual truths as he taught the multitudes of people who followed him. Jesus spoke in the common, everyday language of the people, and he tried to make his teachings accessible to the average person. These teachings and the stories of his miracles are recorded in the four Gospels of the New Testament.

Yet although Jesus ministered to crowds of thousands, the primary focus of his ministry was to a few select people: his disciples. The Jesus "movement" was not the result of crowds following Jesus. Instead, it started with these twelve men. In his classic book *The Master Plan of Evangelism*, Robert Coleman says that Jesus' plan of reproducing disciples "was not with programs to reach the multitudes but with men whom the multitudes would follow . . . Men were to be His method of winning the world to God. The initial objective of Jesus' plan was to enlist men who could bear witness to His life and carry on His work after He returned to the Father."[3] Jesus was intentionally selective in whom he chose to follow him, to instruct and train others and, in time, reproduce what he passed along to them. A few strategic followers who knew his teachings and his practices well—this was Jesus' master plan for launching a movement of reproducing disciples.

From Jesus and his followers, the Christian movement became a contagious multiplication movement. Today there are followers on every continent. Like an epidemic, a contagious movement spreads like an infectious disease from one person to another individual. Every epidemic starts small—with just one or two people—and then, over time, reaches a tipping point and begins to spread rapidly. In the book of Acts, Luke records that there were 120 men and women gathering in Jerusalem thirty days after the death and resurrection of Jesus Christ. Soon afterward, Luke tells us that three thousand additional people were added to these numbers on the Day of Pentecost (Acts 2:41). Since we don't have firm numbers after the records in Acts, scholars have estimated that in the following years Christianity continued to grow at a rate of 40 percent each decade. This means there would have been 7,530 Christians in the year AD 100, followed by 217,795 Christians in AD 200, and 6,299,832 Christians by AD 300.[4]

In studying the earliest days of the Christian movement, researchers and sociologists have sought to understand the factors that contributed to this pattern of continued growth.[5] In other words: *how* did this tiny religious sect originating in the Middle East grow to be the largest religious movement in history? The answer may surprise you.

Sociologist Rodney Stark summarizes the *how* behind the growth of early Christianity by pointing to its spread through interpersonal relationships:

"Christianity did not grow because of miracle working in the market place . . . the primary means of its growth was through the united and motivated efforts of the growing number of believers, who invited their friends, relatives, and neighbors to share the "good news."[6]

Similarly, author and theologian Alan Kreider argues that the improbable rise of Christianity is due to what he refers to as "patient ferment," a phrase pointing to a combination of multiple factors influencing growth over time rather than a single magic bullet that unlocked growth. As Kreider writes, the growth of the early Christian movement "was uncoordinated, it was unpredictable, and it seemed unstoppable. The ferment was spontaneous, and it involved ordinary ingredients that at times synergized into a heady brew."[7]

Stark and Kreider both agree that the surprising growth of the early church lacked a coordinated effort or strategic plan. Rather, the surprising growth of Christianity was the result of the simple, yet life-changing message of the gospel transforming the ordinary lives of the early Christians who patiently and faithfully followed Jesus daily. The message of Jesus shared from person to person over time. This is what contributed, more than anything else, to the steady and rapid spread of Christianity around the world.

The Rise of Global Christianity

The growth of Christianity was not an isolated phenomenon limited to the first few centuries. The history of Christianity is the story of several multiplication movements that cross cultural, language, and geographic boundaries, one following another over time.[8] And while there is much we can learn from the first fifteen hundred years of cross-cultural growth, some of the richest insights for us today come from looking closer at our own Western context and studying the growth of the movement over the last five hundred years. Over time, Christianity spread from the Middle East into the Western hemisphere, eventually taking Europe by storm. From there it followed the pattern of colonial expansion and began to take root in North and South America.

The past five hundred years of church history has often focused on these European churches and their descendants. Yet as historian Phillip Jenkins has noted, the last one hundred years has seen a new shift in the center of gravity for the Christian movement southward to Africa, Asia, and Latin America.[9] Today, the church is growing at an explosive rate throughout the world.[10] Consider the following statistics: In 1910, about two-thirds of the world's Christians lived in Europe, where the bulk of Christians had lived for almost a millennium. Today, over one hundred years later, around one in every four Christians lives in sub-Saharan Africa (24%), and about one in eight is found in Asia and the Pacific (13%). The sheer number of Christians around the world has quadrupled in the last hundred years, from around 600 million in 1910 to more than two billion in 2010. More than 1.3 billion Christians now live in the Global South (61%), compared with about 860 million in the Global North (39%).[11]

This growth and the geographic and cultural shifts we see are happening as a result of various multiplication movements among different people groups. There is much we can learn from the global church by observing what God is doing through these movements. As John Stott suggests, "We must be global Christians with a global vision because our God is a global God."[12] One example of the effect these shifts are having on the movement of Christianity is in the flow of evangelism from culture to culture. Because of the growth of Christianity in the Global South, the flow of evangelism is beginning to reverse from the direction of the recent past. Whereas Western churches were once sending out missionaries and evangelists to reach churches in Africa, Asia, and Latin America, today we are seeing believers from these cultures coming to Europe and North America to re-evangelize the Western world with the gospel of Jesus Christ. British author Martin Robinson speaks of missionaries from nations like Brazil, Haiti, Mexico, Nigeria, Dominican Republic, and Ethiopia, to name a few.[13] As these shifts continue, churches in the West will need to re-examine their old paradigms and adapt to these new movements of God, perhaps through a humble willingness to learn from our brothers and sisters in the wider global church.

These shifts are also leading Western churches to rethink their approach to evangelism within their own cultural context. "Welcome to life on the fastest growing mission field in the world: North America," proclaimed Timothy C. Tennent, president of Asbury Theological Seminary, to incoming seminary students in 2016.[14] Churches in North America and Europe are not witnessing a growing number of people who are radically unchurched or, as Professor Alvin Reid has said, "those who have no clear personal understanding of the message of the gospel, and who have had little or no contact with a Bible-teaching, Christ-honoring church."[15] In the United States alone, there are 180 million who have no connection to a local church, making the United States the largest mission field in the Western Hemisphere and the third largest mission field on Earth.[16]

How should we respond to the dramatic decline of the church in the West? Can the West be won *again*? I believe the answer is yes, but it will take a movement of historic proportions. What might such a multiplication movement look like for us today?

PROFILE

Characteristics of Renewal Movements

In the same way there are a variety of social movements, there are also numerous Christian renewal movements proliferating around the world. For the purposes of this book, we will be looking at the Wesleyan revival as a renewal movement. Thus, it is good to ask the question, "What are common characteristics of renewal movements?" Dr. Howard Snyder has done significant research and writing on the characteristics of renewal movements and has written one of the best books I have read on the subject titled *Signs of the Spirit: How God Reshapes the Church*. In *Signs of the Spirit*, Snyder analyzes church renewal from a historical perspective, focusing on the common features of the Montanist, Pietist, Moravian, and Methodist movements.

Snyder describes a renewal movement as a "sociologically and theologically definable religious resurgence which arises and remains within, or in continuity with, historic Christianity, and which has a significant (potentially measurable) impact on the larger church in terms of number of adherents, intensity of belief and commitment, and/or the creation or revitalization of institutional expressions of the church."[17] This definition will help us frame and understand the Wesleyan revival as a renewal movement within the Church of England.

So how does renewal come to the church? According to Snyder, renewal is often multidimensional. He identifies five dimensions of renewal which offer a framework for understanding how God brings renewal to the church in movements.

1. *Personal Renewal.* When we think of renewal, we usually mean *personal* spiritual renewal. Whatever else renewal is, it surely must be personal. Renewing individual believers is only part of the story, however. God wants to see the whole body of Christ renewed.

2. *Corporate Renewal.* We may call the broader renewing work of the Spirit *corporate renewal*, or the renewal of the whole body. God wants to renew his church as a whole, so that the whole community of believers takes on a renewed life.

3. *Conceptual Renewal.* Renewal may also come *conceptually*, as God provides fresh vision of what the church can and should be. Conceptual renewal is a new vision for the church's life and mission. It comes primarily in the area of our thoughts, ideas, and images of the church.

4. *Structural Renewal.* A fourth dimension of renewal has to do with *forms and structures*. It is the dimension of renewal concerned with the way we, as believers, live out our lives together. It is the question of the best wineskins for the new wine. Renewal often dies prematurely for lack of effective structures.

5. *Missiological Renewal.* A fifth dimension of renewal is *missiological renewal*—the renewal of the church's sense of calling and passion. A church in need of renewal is focused inward. A renewed

church focuses outward to mission and service in the world. Renewal must reach the missiological level in order to be biblically dynamic. A church is not truly renewed until it discovers its mission in the world.[18]

Snyder's work offers a helpful overview of the dynamics of renewal movements and how they work. As we begin to look at the Wesleyan movement in the next few chapters, we will see similarities to Snyder's list and find insights to help us understand what such a movement could look like in our day.

Six Marks of the Wesleyan Movement

As much as we want to see a multiplication movement today, most of us are unable to envision what that might look like. We are familiar with the status quo, the existing models of church that are largely focused on group gatherings for worship and teaching. To begin to clarify our vision, we can benefit from a closer look at church history. There is no better example of a successful church multiplication movement in the West than the Methodist movement of the eighteenth and nineteenth centuries. I believe it serves as an indispensable paradigm for how we can multiply today's church.

Some of you reading this may enjoy lists. Personally, I am not a fan of lists because they may wrongly imply a specific sequence or order of events. Others will assume they are comprehensive, definitively covering all that needs to be said on a subject. For the sake of this book, however, I have developed a list of the six essential marks of the Wesleyan revival, marks that have some correlation to the marks of other renewal movements.

These six marks provide a *genetic* structure—much like the DNA in a living organism—mutually working together to create the movement dynamics that led to the Wesleyan revival. As you read through them, think of them as an interconnected ecosystem rather than focusing on the individual parts. And I want to emphasize that this list is neither authoritative or comprehensive. Rather, it is designed to offer you a simple and accessible snapshot of the key elements that made the Wesleyan revival such a success. As you read them, consider how they might be applied today.

CHANGED LIVES

Movements begin as people's lives are changed by a fresh encounter with the living God. Movements often begin with a catalytic leader like John Wesley, Jonathan Edwards, or William Seymour whose life has been touched by God. Sometimes the change is a conversion experience. At other times it is a personal renewal that results in a radical commitment to follow Christ. Movements are not primarily about numbers or slogans, but about changed lives that lead to broader cultural transformation. In renewal movements, there is usually a tipping point where the transformation occurring in the lives of individuals as they embrace a vision for renewal begins to spread like wildfire, leading to broader social and cultural change.

CONTAGIOUS FAITH

Movements become contagious when ordinary people share their faith with others. One of the reasons a movement grows and spreads is because it has a simple, life-changing message that ordinary people can easily understand and share with others. Revival can spread as people rediscover the simplicity of the gospel or an essential aspect of the Christian faith that inspires and mobilizes them to action. A common feature of these revival movements is an invitation to commit or join a cause, which is effective in helping recruit others to join the movement. In Christian movements, this growth often results from a renewed passion to share the gospel with others, and this passion spreads from one person to another like a contagion. During the Wesleyan revival, while Wesley and other leaders were effective in preaching to large crowds, it was ordinary men and women who were most effective in spreading the Christian message across England and into North America, resulting in the faith of millions of new believers.

THE HOLY SPIRIT

Movements emphasize the person and work of the Holy Spirit in peoples' lives. Fresh encounters with the Holy Spirit create a renewed sense of spiritual vitality among the followers of Christ which leads to personal and corporate renewal. More specifically, the reciprocity of the Word and the Spirit interacting together offers a potent mix that renews peoples' faith and compels them outward to engage the world in mission. The Word of God becomes the foundational authority and guide for life, while the Holy Spirit fills and empowers people to live holy lives and to share their faith with others.

DISCIPLESHIP SYSTEMS

Movements develop systems for discipleship and spiritual growth. This frequently looks like some form of small group structure to facilitate ongoing spiritual growth and commitment. As he preached to large crowds, Wesley quickly discovered that preaching alone was not enough; people needed ongoing support, community, and structure to help them continue on the spiritual journey. To remedy this, he developed a holistic ecosystem designed to help people grow at every stage of their journey. This involved an interlocking discipleship group structure. Each of these structures gathered people into groups of different sizes focused on different aspects of the discipleship process in order to help individuals grow in their faith. There were also spiritual practices that undergirded and reinforced the entire discipleship system.

APOSTOLIC LEADERSHIP

Movements have an apostolic impulse—drawn from the models and methods of the early church—that empowers and mobilizes all of God's people for mission. John Wesley and the early Methodists were not trying to be innovative or original. They drew their inspiration from the faith and spirituality of the early church, especially the church of the first two centuries (the pre-Constantine era). Methodism has been referred to as a lay apostolic movement within the Church of England, which alludes to the recovery of ministry for every Christian believer, not just the ordained leadership.[19] The apostolic impulse of the early church to spread the gospel and plant new churches moved the early Methodists to develop ways to empower and release every member of the body of Christ to use their gifts and talents for God. Wesley personally worked to empower thousands of laity, many who later became leaders of the movement. These ordinary, non-ordained Christian men and women became the foundation of the next generation as the movement spread across the Western world in the eighteenth and nineteenth centuries.

ORGANIC MULTIPLICATION

Movements have an outward missional focus that naturally leads to the multiplication of disciples and new communities of faith. Movements don't become movements by naval gazing, but by looking outward, by inviting people in, and by growing and multiplying its mission and influence. There is a natural dynamism and excitement among the people that makes them contagious, helping the movement spread widely and organically from one person to another. We can describe the growth of movements as organic because it tends to happen naturally, rather than being forced by the leadership at the top level. Movements look outward and grow and multiply as people's lives are changed, they begin making disciples, and then start new ministries and communities of faith to facilitate the ongoing growth of more individuals.

Conclusion

I have introduced these six marks because they form the basis for the remaining chapters of this book. In each of the following chapters, we will look more closely at one of the marks, studying the past in order to uncover how that mark contributed to multiplication and discipleship during the Wesleyan revival. Then we'll consider what we can learn from this for today, asking how we might apply these insights in our own context and culture.

To start connecting the dots between the six marks, we now turn our attention to John Wesley and the Methodist movement. By looking to the past, we will better understand how God brought revival, first to an individual and a group of his close friends, then to the nation of England, eventually forming a worldwide movement. We will begin with John Wesley, learning what we can from his life and experience, and seeing how a fresh encounter with God was the spark that began it all.

CHAPTER 2

CHANGED LIVES

I felt my heart strangely warmed.
JOHN WESLEY

Church history is full of stories of persons who had a life-transforming experience with the risen Christ that left them forever changed. As Steve Addison asserts in his book *Movements That Change the World,* "History is made by men and women of faith who have met with the living God."[1]

Moses met with God at the burning bush.
Paul encountered Christ on the road to Damascus.
Augustine encountered God under a tree.
Luther encountered Christ in the Bible.
Saint Francis encountered God at the cross.
Saint Patrick encountered God in a dream.

And as we will see, John Wesley encountered Christ at Aldersgate. As with most movements, the Methodist revival began with a catalytic leader who experienced a life-changing encounter with God, one that resulted in a rediscovery of the gospel. For some leaders, this encounter is best described as a conversion experience, while for others it is a call to a deeper commitment to the Christ they have already known or met.

Born on June 17, 1703 in the small town of Epworth in northern England, John Wesley was one of Samuel and Susanna Wesley's nineteen children. His family had a wonderful heritage of ministry: his father was a parish priest; his parents were children of clergy; and even the previous generation included an individual in ordained ministry. It seemed natural that Wesley would follow in the footsteps of his father, grandfather, and great-grandfather and commit his life to the service of the Lord.

Wesley's early years at Epworth left a deep impression upon him. Under the teaching and discipleship of his parents, he developed a love for the church and education and devotion to God. Many historians believe his mother, Susanna, had an even stronger influence upon Wesley than his father. Susanna was well read, especially in religious literature, and she kept up the household, taught and disciplined the children, and even held prayer meetings in the rectory when her husband was away. Upon his mother's death in 1742, Wesley recollected, "I cannot but further observe, that even she (as well as her father, and grandfather, her husband, and her three sons) had been, in her measure and degree, a preacher of righteousness."

A life-altering event occurred just before midnight on February 9, 1709, when a fire started in the rectory. Without a moment to lose, most of the family escaped down the staircase and out a door. A few jumped out an upper-story window. To his dismay, after escaping the home, Samuel realized five-year-old

Wesley was still asleep inside. Samuel tried to get back in, but the fire had intensified, and it was impossible to reenter. At the very last minute, a man who had arrived on the scene was able to climb on someone's shoulders and reach up to rescue Wesley from the fire. Almost as soon as he escaped, the entire house burned to the ground. After this, Wesley's mother called him a "brand plucked out of the burning," and the experience was one Wesley would never forget. He remembered it as evidence of the providence of God, who saved him from the fire.

Wesley's Training

As Wesley grew to be a man, he developed a reputation for deep piety, learning, and practical wisdom. His formal education began at the age of eleven when he was sent to Charterhouse, a school that would prepare him for Oxford University. Six years later, in 1720, he matriculated into Christ Church College, Oxford and by the time of his graduation in 1724, he had become well-versed in theology, science, history, and classical literature. While at Oxford, Wesley showed nothing but a seminal interest in religious matters and had little interest in inward religious experiences. After leaving Oxford, however, his thoughts about the nature of religion began to change. Scholars often mark the year 1725 as the start of Wesley's religious awakening and the beginning of the first of three phases in his theological development. He began thinking seriously about becoming an ordained Anglican priest, and his parents enthusiastically encouraged him in this pursuit.

Several factors helped to shape Wesley's religious thought life during this time. First, Wesley was exposed to the following writings, which had a profound impact upon his spirituality:

Bishop Jeremy Taylor's *Rules and Exercises of Holy Living and Dying*, Thomas à Kempis's *Imitation of Christ*, and William Law's *Christian Perfection* and *A Serious Call*. The reading of these books began a process of internalizing his religious beliefs, leading him down the path of holiness. He took communion every week, attended prayers, avoided outward sins, and sought to live a holy life. Wesley was ordained a deacon in September 1725, and became a priest in July 1728.

The Holy Club

At roughly the same time as Wesley, his younger brother, Charles, also entered Christ Church College as a student. Charles helped organize a small group of Oxford students who met regularly for the purpose of study and spiritual formation, and Wesley joined the group. He was quickly recognized as the unofficial leader. It's important to recognize here that while Oxford was formally dedicated to training young men for ministry in the Church of England, it was not a particularly spiritual place. As a student, Charles commented, "Christ Church is certainly the worst place in the world to begin a reformation; a man stands a very fair chance of being out of his religion."[2] However, in God's providence, Oxford would prove to be quite formative for Wesley, Charles, and several others. Along with their academic pursuits, the students were devotedly engaged in prayer, Bible study, fasting, communion, and social work, including prison visitation and caring for the sick. Biographer C. E. Vulliamy describes the Holy Club this way:

> The members of the club spent an hour, morning and evening, in private prayer. At nine, twelve, and three o'clock they

recited a collect, and at all times they examined themselves closely, watching for signs of grace and trying to preserve a high degree of religious fervor. They made use of pious ejaculations, they frequently consulted their Bibles, and they noted, in cipher [that is, coded] diaries, all the particulars of their daily employment. One hour each day was set apart for meditation. They fasted twice a week, observed all the feasts of the church, and received the sacraments every Sunday. Before going into company, they prepared their conversation, so that words might not be spoken without purpose. The primitive church, in so far as they had knowledge of it, was taken as their pattern.[3]

The visibility of these holy practices earned them several nicknames, including "Sacramentarians," "Enthusiasts," "Bible Moths," "Holy Club," and "Methodists." This last name would be the one to stick, eventually becoming the name of the movement. The Wesley brothers also connected with George Whitefield, who would later become another leader in the spreading evangelical revival. Whitefield was a fellow student and also a member of the "Holy Club," and Wesley was impressed with Whitefield's wit and piety. The two men became close friends.

The experiences with the Holy Club mark Wesley's time at Oxford and were an important season of religious development for him and his brother. It was at Oxford that Wesley began to develop his vision for the recovery of "Scriptural Christianity," which would become a distinctive hallmark of the Methodist movement. The combination of personal piety, spiritual discipline, intimate community, and ministry to the poor and sick—all present in seed form in the Holy Club—became the foundation for the Wesleyan movement as it spread throughout England and across the Atlantic.

Wesley's First Trip to America

In 1735, only eight weeks after his father's death, Wesley set sail for Savannah, Georgia. He had accepted the chaplaincy of governor James Oglethorpe in the American colony of Georgia and had been commissioned there as a missionary by the Society for the Propagation of the Gospel, the missionary wing of the Church of England. After a two-month trip by sea, Wesley landed in the colonies on February 6, 1736. While his primary intention in coming to America was ministry to the Native Americans, he found himself serving instead as parish minister to the colonists living in Savannah. His brother, Charles, had accompanied him and was serving as the personal secretary to governor James Oglethorpe. Oglethorpe had been a personal friend of their father, and he was anxious to have Samuel's two sons' help in Georgia.

The mission work of the Wesley brothers in Savannah lasted less than two years.[4] Their ambitions were never fully realized, as Charles's relationship with Oglethorpe was strained from the beginning, and Wesley's dreams of evangelizing the Native Americans were never fulfilled. Instead, he labored tirelessly among the colonials and fell in love with one of his parishioners, Sophy Hopkey. A brief relationship followed, but Wesley was not able to propose, and Sophy was engaged to another man. Five months after the marriage, Wesley refused to serve the new Mrs. Sophy Williamson communion, and the Williamsons sued him for defamation of character. After several stressful months of ministry, Wesley realized his time was over. He wrote in his journal, "I saw clearly the hour was come for leaving this place."

During his time in Georgia, and again on his return to England, Wesley became acquainted with a group of Christian believers called the Moravians. The Moravians were pietists, emphasizing personal practices of prayer and an individual experience of God. They were associated with the teachings of Count Nicholas Ludwig von Zinzendorf, who taught a simple faith and the assurance of salvation through the inner witness of the Spirit. Wesley was impressed with their confidence and how they practiced their faith. On February 7, 1736, while Wesley was still ministering in Georgia, a Moravian leader by the name of August Gottlieb Spangenburg began to respectfully question Wesley's own faith. Wesley later recounted the dialogue:

> He said, "My brother, I must first ask you one or two questions. Have you the witness within yourself? Does the Spirit of God bear witness with your spirit, that you are a child of God?" I was surprised, and knew not what to answer. He observed it and asked, "Do you know Jesus Christ?" I paused, and said, "I know he is Savior of the world." "True," replied he; "but do you know he has saved you?" I answered, "I hope he has died to save me." He only added, "Do you know yourself?" I said, "I do." But I fear they were vain words.[5]

Wesley would later credit the Moravians as instrumental in leading him to search for an inward Christianity, an understanding and experience of God that resulted in a transformed heart and life. On his journey back to England, Wesley wrote, "I went to America to convert the Indians; but oh, who shall convert me? Who is he that will deliver me from this evil heart of unbelief?" It is clear these questions were the result of Wesley comparing his own faith with the simple assurance he had seen among the Moravians. Wesley's longing for a real experience of God and a confident faith would soon come.

A Heart Strangely Warmed

When he returned to England, Wesley spent several months in spiritual distress and deep introspection, challenged by the simple faith in Christ he had witnessed among the Moravians. Then Wesley met another Moravian believer by the name of Peter Böhler. Böhler convinced Wesley that conversion happens in an instant rather than via a long process, and that real Christians have assurance of their salvation from the inner witness of the Holy Spirit. Böhler testified that this was his own experience and presented Wesley with several witnesses who testified to a similar experience of instantaneous faith.

As Böhler shared about the mercies of God, Wesley wept and determined that he would seek his own full assurance of salvation. He wrote, "I was now thoroughly convinced and, by the grace of God, I resolved to seek it unto the end, first, by absolutely renouncing all dependence, in whole or in part, upon my own works of righteousness—on which I had really grounded my hope of salvation, though I knew it not, from my youth up."[6] Clearly, the Moravians had a significant impact on Wesley, his faith, and his understanding of conversion. British Methodist scholar Herbert McGonigle asserts: "No group of Christians had helped John Wesley more sincerely or more profoundly than the Moravians."[7]

Wesley's journal entries from April 2 through May 24, 1738 also provide evidence of a profound shift, showing that the Moravians were instrumental in leading him to search for an inward Christianity of the heart that was accompanied by the inner witness of the Spirit. From the Moravians he learned a new understanding of faith, assurance, and Christian experience, all rooted in the experiential work of the Holy Spirit. The lasting influence of the Moravians can be seen in Wesley's concept of the "witness of the Spirit" which is found throughout his writings and sermons. Then, on May 24, 1738, while attending a prayer meeting at Aldersgate Street in London, John Wesley had his own personal encounter with Jesus Christ, an experience that forever changed his life. He wrote,

> In the evening, I went very unwillingly to a society in Aldersgate Street, where one was reading Luther's Preface to the Epistle to the Romans. About a quarter before nine, while he was describing the change which God works in the heart through faith in Christ, I felt my heart strangely warmed. I felt I did trust in Christ, Christ alone, for salvation; and an assurance was given me that he had taken away my sins, even mine, and saved me from the law of sin and death.
>
> I began to pray with all my might for those who had in a more especial manner despitefully used me and persecuted me. I then testified openly to all there what I now first felt in my heart. But it was not long before the enemy suggested, "This cannot be faith; for where is thy joy?" Then was I taught that peace and victory over sin are essential to faith in the Captain of our salvation; but that, as to the transports of joy that usually attend the beginning of it, especially in those who have mourned deeply, God sometimes giveth, sometimes withholdeth, them according to the counsels of His own will.
>
> After my return home, I was much buffeted with temptations, but I cried out, and they fled away. They returned again and again. I as often lifted up my eyes, and He "sent me help from his holy place." And herein I found the difference between this and my former state chiefly consisted. I was striving, yea, fighting with all my might under the law, as well as under grace. But then I was sometimes, if not often, conquered; now, I was always conqueror."[8]

Some interpreters refer to this experience as Wesley's "conversion." This fresh encounter with God at Aldersgate was significant, however, in preparing Wesley for his next season of ministry as the leader of the growing Methodist movement. However, Aldersgate proved to be just one of many revolutionary milestones in Wesley's religious life that changed the course of his ministry. Albert Outler wrote, speaking of Wesley's later reflections on this event, "It is as if Wesley came to realize that Aldersgate had been *one* in a series of the 'turning points' in his passage from don to missionary to evangelist."[9]

To fully understand Wesley's journey of faith, we must take into consideration the various stages and influences, and not just the Aldersgate experience. What truly formed Wesley into a leader of a movement was a lifetime of study, habits, relationships, and encounters with God. So what were the influences which led to that pivotal moment at Aldersgate? As we look at the life of Wesley, the first major influence was his family, especially his mother on his early faith development. At home in those early years Wesley began to learn about God and first developed a passion for study. His later studies and experiences at Oxford formed the discipline and practices that would carry him the rest of his life. His interaction with the Moravians cultivated in him the hunger for a deeper walk with God, marked by assurance of faith. Through the Moravians he was also introduced to the concept of *band meetings*, small groups of believers meeting for prayer, discussion, spiritual accountability, and encouragement. All of these factors lead us to his Aldersgate experience, which gave him the firm resolve and renewed faith in God that was necessary to lead a movement. Aldersgate was not an isolated event; rather, other members of the early Methodist movement experienced a similar movement of God's presence and power in their lives. Wesley's brother Charles had an experience like

Aldersgate only three days before. Another contemporary of John Wesley, John Newton beautifully demonstrates the magnificent power of encountering God and saving grace.

Newton was born in London on July 24, 1725, the son of a commander of a merchant ship that sailed the Mediterranean. At age eleven, Newton went to sea with his father and began the life of a seaman. He faced many trials at sea and eventually became captain of his own ship, which was involved in the slave trade.

In 1748 Newton had a spiritual conversion while sailing back to England aboard a merchant ship. The vessel encountered a severe storm and almost sank. Newton awoke in the middle of the night and called out to God as the ship was filling with water. After making it through the storm, Newton began to pray and read the Bible for the remainder of the journey. He later marked this experience as the beginning of his conversion to Christianity.

Newton eventually left the slave trade and became an ordained minister in the Church of England, an abolitionist, and beloved hymn writer. Among Newton's contributions is the hymn "Amazing Grace," which is still sung by millions of people throughout the world. "Amazing Grace" beautifully describes God's free grace in song:

Amazing grace!
How sweet the sound
That saved a wretch like me!
I once was lost, but now am found,
Was blind, but now I see.
'Twas grace that taught my heart to fear,
And grace my fears relieved;
How precious did that grace appear,
The hour I first believed!

Thro' many dangers, toils and snares,
I have already come;
'Tis grace has brought me safe thus far,
And grace will lead me home.

PROFILE

Martin Luther and the Spark of the Reformation

Over two hundred years before Wesley, Martin Luther encountered the grace of God. Luther was born November 10, 1483 in Eisleben, Germany. After almost dying in a lightning storm, Luther joined the monastery of the Augustinian Order in Erfurt where strict discipline was expected and enforced. He gave himself completely to the rigorous monastic life of prayer, study, and the daily practice of the sacraments, and regularly confessed his sins to a priest. He was trying to earn his salvation through good works, but nothing would satisfy his inner longing for acceptance from God.

Luther became a full-time professor at the University of Wittenberg, where he taught theology and the Bible. There he began to study the books of Romans and Galatians. These two New Testament writings helped him discover the doctrine of justification by faith and salvation by grace. After years of wrestling with God, Martin Luther finally accepted the grace of God. He beautifully described his personal experience of justification by faith in the following way:

Night and day I pondered until I saw the connection between the justice of God and the statement that "the just shall live by his faith." Then I grasped that the justice of God is that righteousness by which through grace and sheer mercy God justifies us through faith. Thereupon I felt myself to be reborn and to have gone through open doors into paradise. The whole of Scripture took on a new meaning, and whereas before the "justice of God" had filled me with hate, now it became to me inexpressibly sweet in greater love."[10]

Luther's encounter with God was the spark that marked the beginning of the Protestant Reformation and the rediscovery of the doctrine of justification by grace through faith alone.

It was while hearing Luther's Preface to the Epistle to the Romans that Wesley encountered God at Aldersgate. Like Luther, Wesley's experience gave him an assurance of his faith and a firm belief in the grace of God and the courage to become the leader of a movement. The two men's encounters with God caused their faith to evolve from mere theory to tangible experience with the living God.

Following Jesus Today

As stated earlier, Wesley's encounter with God at Aldersgate was not an isolated experience. People still encounter God today, often in powerful experiences of grace and conviction. I can attest to this firsthand. At the age of nineteen, I began to search for answers to the meaning of life, questioning the existence of God. Unlike Wesley, I had little personal experience with church growing up. Yet for the first time in my life, as I sought and questioned, I had a growing awareness of my own sin and personal need for God. I began to sense that there was more to life than the way I was living, because the way I was living only brought me misery and pain. I remember one day in particular when I felt compelled to go to the lake near my house to think about these things. Little did I know that this moment would become a crossroads experience in my life, similar to Wesley's experience at Aldersgate. Sitting on a rock near the lake, I broke down in tears and spoke openly to God, confessing my desire to turn from my destructive ways. Immediately, I experienced the presence and the peace of God in my heart and life. Like Wesley, I felt my heart strangely warmed and the love of God flooded my soul, and I felt as if the guilty stain of my sins had been washed away. Sitting at the edge of the water, I accepted Jesus Christ into my heart as my Lord and Savior. I have been following Jesus since that day and continue doing so after all these years.

I share this because my story is not unique. In my work as a pastor, church planter, and professor, I have met hundreds of people from all over the United States and around the world whose lives have been changed by similar encounters with Jesus Christ. They come from different backgrounds and stages of life; some are poor, while others are millionaires. But what each has in common is a simple faith and trust in Jesus Christ as their Lord and Savior. When Jesus calls a person, he demands a response, and the call of God cannot be ignored or go unanswered. Either the hearer will trust and obey or doubtfully deny. But whatever the answer, we must respond to the call.

And what is the call of God? German theologian and pastor Dietrich Bonhoeffer once said, "When Christ calls a man, he bids him come and die."[11] The call to follow Christ, first and foremost, is a call to total self-surrender. We must leave behind our self-dependence and resolve to follow Jesus, just as the disciples did in their day. We may not understand every doctrine of the Christian faith, but we must know that the one we are following demands and deserves our allegiance as the Son of God. As C. S. Lewis has said, a person must either accept the claims of the Bible in faith or dismiss them entirely—there is no middle ground:

> A man who was merely a man and said the sort of things Jesus said would not be a great moral teacher. He would either be a lunatic—on the level with a man who says he is a poached egg—or he would be the Devil of Hell. You must make your choice. Either this man was, and is, the Son of God: or else a madman or something worse. You can shut Him up for a fool, you can spit at Him and kill Him as a demon; or you can fall at His feet and call Him Lord and God. But let us not come with any patronizing nonsense about His being a great human teacher. He has not left that open to us. He did not intend to.[12]

How are we to respond to Jesus? Each of us must decide for ourselves whether Jesus is Lord, a liar, or a lunatic. Either he is the Son of God, or he is not. I have known many wonderful people who have wanted to believe the things Jesus said and taught, but they could not affirm his divine identity.

Every journey begins with a first step. Becoming a Christian is simple, yet deeply profound. It begins with God's free offer of salvation through his Son, Jesus Christ. If you are not a believer, what you must do to believe is put your faith and hope in Jesus

Christ as Lord and Savior. As I said, it is simple, but it is not easy! Instead of trusting in ourselves, we place our trust in Christ alone to save us from our sin and fallen nature through the work he has accomplished on the cross. Surrender your life to him today and begin to follow him! As we have seen with Wesley, and as I can personally attest, God does extraordinary things through ordinary people who surrender their life to him.

I share this because *this* is the stuff that movements are made of. Every Christian revival movement begins with a follower of Christ making a radical commitment to follow Jesus. This is the beginning point and foundation. But be forewarned: being a follower of Jesus is not for the faint of heart! Following Jesus does not eliminate life's problems or difficulties. On the contrary, as a believer you will likely have to suffer for your faith. Your commitment to Christ will be resisted and attacked in one form or another, as all Christians are called to identify with Christ's mission, which inevitably involves suffering and possibly death. This does not mean that every believer will necessarily have to die for their faith, but we must be willing and ready to lay down our lives for the Lord. As disciples of Jesus, we accept whatever may come our way as we follow the mission and share the message of Christ. If we are to have any hope of a revival movement in our day, it will begin with ordinary believers having a fresh encounter with the living Christ.

Conclusion

Stories of people like John Wesley, Martin Luther, and John Newton remind us that God works through ordinary people. And people are still encountering the living God today. Although Wesley believed many truths about God, it wasn't until he had a living encounter with Jesus Christ at Aldersgate that he had the full assurance of his faith necessary to shape him to become the leader of the Methodist movement. The stories of men like Luther, Wesley, and Newton teach us that you can know about God without actually *knowing* God. Just because you are a member of a church or were baptized as a child doesn't make you an actual believer. If this was the case, many of the contemporary mainline denominations wouldn't be in such rapid decline. No, this chapter reminds us that we need a life-changing encounter with God. This fresh encounter with the living God was the spark used to change Wesley's life.

But Aldersgate was not the beginning. The start of the movement was nearly two thousand years earlier in the coming of Jesus Christ. Throughout history, God has used many individuals—from the apostle Paul to Augustine of Hippo to Martin Luther and others—and as we shall see in the next chapter, Wesley had not invented something new but simply rediscovered the power of something old. From generation to generation, God never changes: "Jesus Christ is the same yesterday and today and forever" (Hebrews 13:8). This rediscovery of the foundational life-changing encounter with God and the basic beliefs of Christianity laid the foundation for a contagious faith that would spread from person to person across England and into the new world.

CHAPTER 3

A CONTAGIOUS FAITH

In the late eighteenth and nineteenth centuries,
the Methodist movement became an epidemic
in England and North America.
MALCOLM GLADWELL

National best-selling author Malcolm Gladwell has written a thought-provoking book titled *The Tipping Point: How Little Things Can Make a Big Difference.* Gladwell looks at how ideas, trends, and social behaviors spread like wildfire once they reach a tipping point, beyond which the multiplication is exponential. He draws several parallels between the spread of ideas, behaviors, and trends and the spread of contagious viruses into devastating epidemics:

The Tipping Point is the biography of an idea, and the idea is very simple. The best way to understand the emergence of fashion trends, the ebb and flow of crime waves, or, for that matter, the transformation of unknown books into best sellers, or the rise of teenage smoking, or the phenomenon of word of mouth, or any number of the other mysterious changes that mark everyday life is to think of them as epidemics. Ideas and products and messages and behaviors spread just like viruses do.[1]

But all of this leads to the question Gladwell poses: "So why is it that some ideas or behaviors or products start epidemics and others don't?" Or to say it another way: "Why do some ideas become movements and other don't?" Though there are many factors involved, Gladwell distills them down to three simple rules: the law of the few, the stickiness factor, and the power of context. The law of the few is the idea that social epidemics are spread by *a handful of exceptional individuals* through their influence and social connections. The stickiness factor suggests there are specific ways of *making a contagious message memorable*, and these methods can make all the difference in how that message spreads and the impact it makes. The power of context says that human beings are strongly influenced by their circumstances and conditions and are particularly *sensitive to the environments in which they live.*[2]

Gladwell's hypothesis, while initially applied to the marketing of products and brands, has relevance for the spread of larger social and religious movements as well. If we consider the three rules identified in Gladwell's analysis and apply them to the Methodist movement, we find immediate parallels. As we will see in this chapter, Wesley had his own "big idea," and he utilized the law of the few to spread it widely among his social network.

Methodism also had a stickiness factor, which spread through contagious relationships that united evangelism and discipleship together. As we will see, the early Methodists understood the power of context, seeking to reach people right where they lived.

As we learned in chapter 1, a movement is an organized network of people with a shared definition of reality, a shared message, and a shared cause with shared objectives. All successful social movements will begin with a clear and simple message, idea, or purpose that unifies people for a common cause. As we apply this filter to Methodism, we discover that the big idea—the "shared definition of reality"—was the core message of salvation. And the shared cause uniting the movement was the communication of this message through field preaching and lay preachers.

The Message of Salvation

With his newfound personal experience of salvation, John Wesley had a burden to share with others that led him to bypass the traditional methods and structures of his day and proclaim the message of salvation directly to the masses. The message of salvation is the scarlet thread woven throughout John Wesley's writings, and it was through this lens that he sought to understand and explain Christian experience in a way ordinary people could understand. The bulk of Wesley's sermons deal with the theme of salvation (*Salvation by Faith*, *Almost Christian*, *Scriptural Christianity*, *The Scripture Way of Salvation*, *Justification by Faith*, *The Marks of the New Birth*, and *The New Birth*, just to name a few). Wesley's theology of salvation was very practical, and he took care to highlight the importance for everyone—man, woman, boy, and girl—to hear the message of salvation. Wesley wanted everyone to experience the transforming power of the gospel, so not only did he preach these marvelous truths, he shared them in his writings, hymns, and journals, publishing them for others to read and re-read. He hoped to put these writings in the hands of every Methodist, so that they would encounter personally the very same truths he was so passionate about.

Wesley also emphasized the necessity of a new birth, a spiritual process sometimes referred to as *regeneration*. This is in keeping with what he had read in John 3:7, "You must be born again." Wesley used the terms "new birth," "born again," and "regeneration" interchangeably to describe this work of God in the human heart, a spiritual birth wherein we are born again. This emphasis on the new birth eventually became a hallmark of the Methodist movement and served as a catalyst for its growth. Wesley found that the simple, life-changing message of the gospel resonated deeply with the heartfelt needs of ordinary people. So he intentionally sought to keep his sermons and writings accessible to the masses: "I design plain truth for plain people: Therefore, of set purpose, I abstain from all nice and philosophical speculations; from all perplexed and intricate reasonings; and, as far as possible, from even the show of learning, unless in sometimes citing the original Scriptures."[3] He believed the life-changing power of the gospel was for everyone; not just the rich or privileged, but for ordinary people.

Field Preaching

As Gladwell pointed out, the tipping point in a movement often occurs when the message begins to spread from person to person like a virus. Having personally experienced a fresh sense of spiritual awakening, many of the early Methodists began to share the gospel with others. They proclaimed the message of salvation through personal evangelism and open-air preaching. This began, in part, because the Wesleys' Oxford friend, George Whitefield, had begun to experience success with field preaching in the United States and England. Whitefield soon became something of a celebrity. He was a gifted orator and could be heard by thousands of people without the aid of a microphone. Benjamin Franklin was one of Whitefield's admirers. Once, when Whitefield was preaching in North America, Franklin worked his way through the crowd using the distance as a base and, counting the number of people within a certain segment, calculated that around thirty thousand people in that location could hear Whitefield.

Whitefield was especially successful preaching to the masses in public sites all around England, including the marketplaces, brickyards, coal pits, and open fields. In Kingswood, as many as twenty thousand coal diggers came out to hear him preach. Whitefield described their response:

> Having no righteousness of their own to renounce, they were glad to hear of a Jesus who was a friend of publicans, and came not to call the righteous, but sinners to repentance. The first discovery of their being affected was to see the white gutters made by their tears which plentifully fell down their black cheeks, as they came out of their coal pits. Hundreds and hundreds of them were soon brought under deep convictions, which, as the event proved, happily ended in a sound and thorough conversion. The change was visible to all, though numbers chose to impute it to anything, rather than the finger of God.[4]

Wesley had been preaching in various parishes, but his

new message of "inward religion" was not received well by the established Church of England, and pulpits soon began closing to him. In April 1739, George Whitefield convinced Wesley that he should begin preaching in the open air in Bristol. At first, Wesley was unconvinced, saying, "I should have thought the saving of souls almost a sin," adding, "if it had not been done in a church [building]."[5] Reluctantly, as Whitefield persisted, Wesley agreed to attempt field preaching. He later reflected on the event in his journal: "I submitted to be more vile, and proclaimed in the highways the glad tidings of salvation, speaking from a little eminence in a ground adjourning to the city about three thousand people."[6] This event marked the beginning of his evangelistic ministry to the masses, as Wesley did more and more preaching outside to large crowds. From this point forward, Wesley began bringing the message of Christ to everyone he came into contact with, driven by a new evangelistic zeal.

A few years later, after he was barred from preaching at his late father's parish church in Epworth, Wesley preached a sermon atop his father's grave with great success. Commenting on this, he remarked, "I am well assured I did far more good to them by preaching three days on my father's tomb than I did by preaching three years in his pulpit."[7] Wesley's embrace of open-air preaching was a key breakthrough, enabling the message to spread more widely and quickly than anyone could have anticipated, and it marked a sharp break with traditional practice. To this point in the history of the Church of England, Anglican clergy rarely, if ever, preached outside the four walls of a church building.

Yet rather than hindering Wesley's ministry, open-air preaching allowed the message to be heard by thousands of ordinary people, many of whom were poor and wouldn't have been welcome in the established churches. Wesley took the message of salvation to the highways and hedges, and the people responded in crowds numbering in the thousands. In every sermon, he emphasized the simple message of salvation, calling for a response from those who listened. "What is the best general method of preaching?" he once asked. "To invite; to convince; to offer Christ; to build up; and to do this in some measure in every sermon."[8]

As the crowds continued to grow, other individuals began open-air preaching as well, and it became necessary for Wesley to develop some guidelines to train other would-be preachers. In 1747, Wesley outlined the following rules for his fellow Methodist preachers to follow:

> Ensure to begin and end precisely at the same time appointed.
>
> Sing no hymns of your own composing.
>
> Endeavour to be serious, weighty, and solemn in your whole deportment before the congregation.
>
> Choose the plainest text you can.
>
> Take care not to ramble from your text, but to keep close to it, and make out what you undertake.
>
> Always suit the subject to the audience.
>
> Beware of allegorizing or spiritualizing too much.
>
> Take care of anything awkward or affect, either in your gestures or pronunciation.
>
> Tell each other if you observe anything of this kind.[9]

These guidelines help paint a picture of Wesley's insight into the need for clear and concise preaching, which made the early Methodist movement so effective among ordinary people. The Methodist message was bringing renewal, and that renewal was spreading among the people through the method of open-air preaching, but the movement was too large for a single individual. Others were needed to spread the message, and this led to the next phase of growth for the movement—the equipping of lay preachers. It was clear a new movement was underway. How would Wesley accomplish the monumental task of reaching the nation? The answer to that question was the training of everyday, ordinary people to share that message. Perhaps the greatest contributing factor to the contagious spread of early Methodism was the changed lives of those who heard the message. Ordinary working men and women had their lives changed by the power of the gospel, and they in turn gave their lives to promoting this "scriptural Christianity" across the land by doing the work that has traditionally been left to ordained priests—the work of evangelism and preaching.

To quote an old English nursery rhyme, these were the "butchers, bakers, and candlestick makers." Wesley began training up non-ordained, non-seminary-trained men and women to be his lay assistants. He taught them to teach others, to evangelize, and to preach. Howard Snyder writes that these lay leaders functioned like a quasi-monastic order: "The itinerary was in fact an order—a preaching order, which, if not celibate, certainly knew about poverty and obedience." [10] The leaders were under Wesley's supervision, and he gave them strict rules, expecting them to preach, study, travel, and meet with small groups of people, as well as exercise daily and eat sparingly.

In 1746, Wesley established a set of guidelines to evaluate those who wanted to become preachers:

Q. *How shall we try those who believe they are moved by the Holy Ghost and called to preach?*
A. Inquire:

1. Do they know in whom they have believed? Have they the love of God in their hearts? Do they desire and seek

nothing but God? And are they holy in all manners of conversation?

2. Have they gifts (as well as grace) for the work? Have they (in some tolerable degree) a clear, sound understanding? Have they a right judgment in the things of God? Have they a just conception of the salvation by faith? And has God given them any degree of utterance? Do they speak justly, readily, clearly?

3. Have they the success? Do they not only speak as generally either to convince or affect the hearts, but have any received remission of sins by their preaching a clear and lasting sense of the love of God? As long as these three marks undeniably concur in any, we allow him to be called of God to preach. These we receive as sufficient reasonable evidence that he is moved thereto by the Holy Ghost.[11]

Most of the ordained Anglican clergy were opposed to these non-traditional practices. As Gerald R. Cragg points out, "Wesley was ridiculed and abused because the eighteenth century was not prepared to tolerate, still less welcome, an ardent evangelical revival."[12] One critic, Augustus Toplady, accused Wesley of "prostituting the ministerial function to the lowest and most illiterate mechanics, persons of almost any class."[13] Wesley defended himself against his critics, pushing back somewhat sarcastically, "Is not a lay preacher preferable to a drunken preacher, to a cursing, swearing preacher?"[14] He said this because, sadly, it was sometimes true of the ordained clergy in the Church of England at the time.

Success rarely comes easy, and it often invites opposition and even persecution. As the movement began to grow, Wesley and his preachers were met with greater opposition. In some cities, mobs vigorously tried to stop the Methodists from speaking and spreading the message of scriptural holiness. Yet time after time,

Wesley's life was spared by divine intervention. There are numerous stories of times when it appeared the crowds might take Wesley's life, but by some odd occurrence he would be spared from harm. On March 19, 1742, Wesley wrote in his journal about a time when persecutors tried to break up his meeting by sending in a bull to disturb his preaching.[15]

Despite persecution, opposition, and hardships, Methodist preachers saw great success in winning converts throughout the British Isles and North America. They burned with missionary zeal as they shared the gospel truth with conviction and obeyed the masters' call to "go into all the world, and preach the gospel to every creature" (Mark 16:15 NKJV). Wesley challenged his preachers to focus on saving souls and emphasizing holiness:

> It is not your business to preach so many times, and to take care of this or that society; but to save as many souls as you can; to bring as many sinners as you can to repentance, and with all your power to build them up in that holiness without which they cannot see the Lord.[16]

The call to spread scriptural Christianity rang out clearly and persisted among generations of Methodists, giving them a sense of urgency to win the lost. Early Methodism spread through a simple strategy: to preach the salvation message to ordinary people everywhere they went. Upon departing to engage in mission work in America, Thomas Coke asked John Wesley what message he should proclaim. Wesley's response: "Offer them Christ." He would later elaborate by emphasizing the importance of going to those in greatest need: "You have nothing to do but to save souls. Therefore spend and be spent in this work. And go not only to those that need you, but to those that need you most."[17]

PROFILE

The Moravian Missionary Movement

Another contagious movement that influenced the Wesleyan revival was the Moravian Missionary Movement. One of the greatest missionary movements of all time, it began with the rich young ruler who said yes. Count Ludwig von Zinzendorf was born into one of the most ancient of noble families in Austria. One eventful day, a Moravian refugee ended up at his door in Dresden. The man's name was Christian David. He had heard that Zinzendorf would open his home to oppressed Moravian refugees. Zinzendorf agreed to the request and a group of ten Moravians arrived in December 1722. His manor became known as "Herrnhut," meaning "the Lord's watch" or "on the watch for the Lord." This was only the beginning. By May 1725, ninety Moravians had settled at Herrnhut. By late 1726, the population had swelled to three hundred.

1727 was an important year, as it marked a spiritual turning point in the Moravian community when a spirit of prayer began to spread among them. They covenanted together to meet often to pour out their hearts in prayer and hymns. On August 5, the count spent the whole night in prayer with about twelve or fourteen others, following a large meeting for prayer at midnight. Then a few days later, on August 13, 1727, the Moravians experienced a powerful "Pentecost" during a communion service when the Spirit came upon Zinzendorf and the community. This experience radically changed the community and sparked a flame of prayer and missions that would burn for decades to come. Looking back on that day, Zinzendorf later recalled, "The whole place represented truly a visible tabernacle of God among men."[18]

This marked the beginning of the Moravian commitment to a round-the-clock "prayer watch" that continued nonstop for over a hundred years. On August 26, 1727, twenty-four men and twenty-four women covenanted together to continue praying in intervals of one hour each, day and night, each hour allocated by lots to different people. Others joined them, and the number increased to seventy-seven. They all carefully observed the hour which had been appointed for them, and they had a weekly meeting where prayer needs were given to them.

Within a short time, Herrnhut became a missionary launching pad that would send out missionaries throughout the world. They assembled small groups of individuals who gathered for prayer and Bible study and who traveled across Europe, sharing the gospel with everyone they met, especially the outcasts of society. Out of this grew a network of small groups that eventually became known as the "Diaspora." Under Zinzendorf's leadership, Moravian missionaries went out into all the world in an unprecedented way.

By the time Zinzendorf died in 1760, after twenty-eight years of cross-cultural mission, the Moravians had sent out 226 missionaries and entered ten different countries. Mission stations had been established in Danish St. Thomas, in the West Indies (1732); Greenland (1733); Georgia, North America (1734); Lapland (1735); Suriname, or Dutch Guiana, on the north coast of South America (1735); Cape Town, South Africa (1737); Elmina, the Dutch headquarters in the Gold Coast (1737); Demarara, now known as Guyana, South America (1738); Jamaica (1754), and Antigua (1756). In 1760 there were forty-nine men and seventeen women serving in thirteen stations around the world, ministering to over six thousand people.

The Moravian passion for mission was grounded in one thing, and one thing alone. Zinzendorf said, "I have but one passion—it is He, it is He alone. The world is the field, and the field is the world; and henceforth that country shall be my home where I can be most used in winning souls for Christ."[19] Over the years, his passion for Jesus grew, as did his passion for the lost. He was determined to evangelize the world through raising up and sending out Moravian missionaries who were equipped only with a simple love for Jesus and the spirit of prayer.

Joining Evangelism and Discipleship

We've established that the Methodist movement spread with a simple but powerful message, utilizing new methods and equipping lay preachers to exponentially multiply. But history is filled with movements that quickly grew, only to collapse just as quickly. What is needed for a movement to persist is a "sticky" factor, something that embeds the message in hearts and minds in a way that sustains the multiplication and growth. By using the word "sticky," I am referring to the connection between ideas and reality, the movement from theory to practice. The Wesleyan revival was, above all things, practical and focused on "plain truths for plain people." Perhaps that is what I love best about Wesley and his movement: it was grounded in reality.

What made the Methodist movement "sticky"? Many believe that the lasting success of the growing movement was due to Wesley's emphasis on *both* evangelism *and* discipleship. Sadly, these activities are not always connected. Even today, some churches focus on evangelism at the expense of discipleship, seeking to win converts instead of making disciples. But Wesley understood what many are recovering again today: the goal of evangelism is disciple-making. Jesus was clear in the Great Commission in Matthew 28 that the church exists to make disciples who will follow Christ, rather than to simply win converts or increase numbers. When Jesus said "make disciples," the disciples understood that this was more than simply getting someone to believe facts or statements about Jesus. They knew that making a disciple meant reproducing in others what Jesus had produced in them. Robert Coleman helpfully explains the Great Commission in this way:

> The Great Commission is not merely to go to the ends of the earth preaching the Gospel (Mark 16:15), nor to baptize a lot of converts into the name of the triune God, nor to teach them the precepts of Christ, but to "make disciples"—to build people like themselves who were so constrained by the commission of Christ that they not only follow, but also lead others to follow His way.[20]

One of the lasting marks of the Wesleyan movement is the recovery of this Great Commission focus on *both* evangelism and discipleship. Although George Whitefield was a masterful preacher who led thousands to repent and put their faith in Christ, he did not have the insight or the leadership genius to place new converts into structured small groups for nurturing and development. Toward the end of his life, Whitefield lamented this fact, saying, "My brother Wesley acted very wisely . . . the souls that were awakened under his ministry he joined in class, and thus preserved the fruits of his labor. This I neglected, and my people are a rope of sand."[21]

Wesley, on the other hand, saw the need for deeper discipleship, and sought to provide those who were converted as part of the Methodist movement with fellowship and accountability. He learned this from his own experience in the Oxford "Holy Club." All who desired to "flee from the wrath to come, and to be saved from their sins" were invited to join discipleship groups.[22] For Wesley, the Christian faith was a social religion—meaning that community was vital—and turning it into a solitary religion would destroy it. So while George Whitefield tended to focus his efforts exclusively on evangelism, Wesley saw that evangelism alone was not enough to sustain a lasting movement. He realized that discipleship and evangelism are two sides of the same coin; they cannot be separated. Evangelism is the beginning of the journey, and discipleship is the ongoing process of spiritual growth.

To unleash the power of this movement dynamic today, the church must recover this emphasis on an integrative process that begins with evangelism and continues with serious disciple-making. The Great Commission is not just leading people to make a decision. If we want to see a multiplication movement today, we must learn from the past. The Wesleyan revival sought to not only make converts, but to make radical disciples of Christ by creating discipleship systems.

Holistic Mission

Finally, evangelism and discipleship is incomplete if it fails to address the whole person with the whole gospel. The Wesleyan revival sought to transform all of society, and especially the lives of the poor. They did this by caring for people's bodies as well as their souls. While Wesley valued "inward religion," he wasn't concerned with the soul of a person alone, but sought to minister to the whole person with the whole gospel. This means that the good news of the gospel is holistic in that it brings the good news to a whole person's body, mind, and soul. Wesley and his brother, Charles, were moved by compassion for the lower classes of society, and for those who were disenfranchised. It was common for Wesley and his preachers to not only minister to the poor, but to regularly dine with them as well. He once said, "I myself as well as the other preachers who are in town, diet with the poor on the same food and at the same table. And we rejoice herein as a comfortable earnest of our eating bread together in our Father's kingdom."[23]

Wesley was not afraid to associate himself with others who stood for human rights causes, including the fight against slavery, support for additional rights for women and children, and the establishment of better labor laws. Wesley wrote a letter to William Wilberforce, who tirelessly fought against slavery in England, in which he said, "O, be not weary in well doing! Go on, in the name of the God and in the power of his might, till even American slavery (the vilest that ever saw the sun) shall vanish away before it."[24] Wesley actively supported several reformist social causes, and he believed that the Methodists were called to be a means of "doing good" to others. He urged his followers to actively participate in meeting the needs of those around them:

By doing good, by being in every kind merciful after their

power; as they have opportunity, doing good of every possible sort, and as far as is possible, to all men: to their bodies, of the ability which God giveth, by giving food to the hungry, by clothing the naked, by visiting or helping them that are sick, or in prison; to their souls by instructing, reproving, or exhorting all they that have intercourse with.[25]

John Wesley practiced what he preached. Though he made fourteen hundred pounds in one year from his book sales, he only kept thirty pounds for himself. He gave much of his money to the poor and to other worthwhile causes, once remarking, "If I leave behind me ten pounds, you and all mankind bear witness against me that I lived and died a thief and a robber."[26] His denial of self and property for the sake of the less fortunate is again reminiscent of the culture and practice of the early church, yet sadly remains uncommon in many North American and European churches today.

Wesley felt that the church had an obligation to care for all of society, but especially for those who could not take care of themselves, and he taught that believers have a social responsibility to the world:

> "Holy Solitaries" is a phrase no more consistent with the Gospel than "holy adulterers." The Gospel of Christ knows of no religion, but social; no holiness, but social holiness. Faith working by love is the length and breadth and depth and height of Christian perfection.[27]

The church is to be the body of Christ for the sake of the world and to offer community for those within the world, especially for those who are less fortunate. This is a natural out-working of faith and discipleship.

Conclusion

In his book *Finding Faith Today: How Does It Happen?* John Finney reports that most people in our Western culture experience their faith primarily through relationships. Individuals encounter the gospel—hearing the message, learning the habits and practices of the community, and growing in faith—through relationships with other believers. Becoming a mature Christian is a process that takes time, and it does not happen in isolation.[28] Finney contends that people come to faith gradually, often beginning with significant relationships with Christian believers, rather than through a sudden decision.[29] Typically, a person is introduced to the faith community through a member of their family, a friendship with a Christian, or through marketplace contact with a minister. After a relationship is established, they begin to ask questions, and they are invited to explore and come to a knowledge and practice of the faith through a small community group. Over time they discover that they have come to embrace the faith through these relationships, and they eventually make a decision to embrace Christ through baptism.[30]

This emphasis on growing in faith in community is a key mark of the Wesleyan way. While Wesley was always ready to invite people to make a decision for Christ, he followed that invitation with a second one, to grow in community with other believers. Again, I believe this needs to be recovered if we hope to see a fresh movement of Christianity in the West. I've seen firsthand how the Christian faith is contagious and can reach unchurched people through relationships.

A man named Adam was the first person who came to faith in our new church. He was a young schoolteacher who did not grow up going to church, and the few times he did attend a church, he was exposed to bad church politics. He came to believe that most Christians are hypocrites. Adam was never exposed to Christianity as a relationship with Jesus, and his experience in community led him to want nothing to do with church.

I met Adam one night at a baseball game. We began to develop a relationship, and I spent several months meeting with him. One day he and his wife showed up at a Christmas service. That morning I was preaching a sermon called "From the Cradle to the Cross" on the significance of the birth of Jesus, and at the conclusion, I invited everyone to respond to the message by welcoming Jesus into their hearts and lives. Adam responded, giving his heart to Jesus Christ, and his life was forever changed.

That's not the end of the story, however. While that event was significant, the real story of Adam's faith is found in the countless hours of one-on-one discipleship that began before that moment and continued long after he came to faith. Very little of that discipleship took place in a church building. We spent time together in coffee shops, at the beach surfing together, and enjoying dinner together with our families. This one-on-one discipleship became a firm foundation for Adam, and over the course of the next five years, Adam's entire family came to faith, including his mother, father, and sister! Years later, he and his family are still walking with Jesus, and they are important leaders in our church and the local community.

For a multiplication movement to sustain growth like this, it must be sticky, and this means a renewed focus on keeping those we reach with the gospel engaged through intentional, relational discipleship. In the next chapter, we will focus our attention on the spiritual fervor of the Methodist movement and how it resulted from the person and work of the Holy Spirit in the lives of the early Methodists.

CHAPTER 4

———•———

THE HOLY SPIRIT

*Pray daily for a great outpouring of the Spirit on
the Church and on the world. This is the grand
need of the day—it is the thing that we need far
more than money, machinery, and men.*

J. C. RYLE

Have you ever been to a concert or sporting event and found yourself swept up in the excitement of the crowd? I was recently eating in a pub in the north of England with a few friends after preaching one Sunday morning at a local church. As we ate and talked about life and ministry, I noticed something odd every few minutes. The normal noise level in the pub would suddenly increase several decibels, erupting with cheers and screams. I thought, *What in the world is happening?* I quickly realized a soccer match was on the television, and all the excitement was because England was winning in the playoffs!

Revival movements are typically marked with a distinct and unmistakable energy, an infectious passion. Most of the growing global Christian movements today have a robust, experiential spirituality that is deeply Spirit-filled and prayerful. Such was the case with early Methodism. The Methodist movement was marked with a fervent spirituality, the result of a strong emphasis on the person and work of the Holy Spirit in the everyday lives of people.[1] In this chapter we will look at the Methodist movement's recovery of the Christian experience and the empowering presence of the Holy Spirit in ordinary life.

Reasonable Enthusiasts

John Wesley and the early Methodists cultivated a fervent spirituality that emphasized a balance between reason and experience. Critics referred to Wesley and the Methodists as "reasonable enthusiasts" because of this dual emphasis.[2] The word *enthusiasm* is derived from the Greek "en-theos" meaning "the God within." It implied a type of "possession by a divine spirit." In the eighteenth century, enthusiasm was often seen as something akin to the possession of evil spirits or a form of hysteria. Though their critics meant the label to be derogatory, in recovering enthusiasm, Wesley and the Methodists were seeking to recover something good that had been lost or forgotten in the practice of the Christian faith. As Paul Chilcote reminds us, "The Wesleys rediscovered this important spiritual law: the church needs enthused disciples. 'Enthused' literally means to be properly filled with God."[3] Wesley believed we need a form of spirituality that is "enthused" in the truest sense of the word—a Spirit-filled faith.

In Wesley's day, much of Christianity was cold and sterile, detached from the emotions and lacking outward expression. Anglican clergy often denounced religious experience and emotion in favor of scientific reason, and John Wesley recognized the need to reappropriate Christian experience. Speaking of the role of experience in Christianity, he said, "a great evangelical truth has been recovered, which had been for many years well-nigh lost and forgotten."[4] Experience was a missing jewel that Wesley rediscovered and placed back into the crown of Christianity.

Just what did Wesley mean when he referred to experience? Christian experience is a personal, firsthand encounter with the living God who gives us the "witness" or "testimony" of the Spirit, which Wesley described in this way: "The testimony of the Spirit is an inward impression of the soul, whereby the Spirit of God directly witnesses to my spirit, that I am a child of God."[5] This inward "impression" on the soul includes our feelings and emotions, but it is far more. It is a complex synergism involving both feelings and intuition, occurring through the work of the Holy Spirit. In "A Letter to a Roman Catholic," Wesley wrote:

> I believe the infinite and eternal Spirit of God, equal with the Father and the Son, to be not only perfectly holy in himself but the immediate cause of all holiness in us; enlightening our understandings, rectifying our wills and affections, renewing our natures, uniting our persons to Christ, assuring us of the adoption of sons, leading us in our actions; purifying and sanctifying our souls and bodies, to a full and eternal enjoyment of God.[6]

The Spirit bears witness with our spirit that we are children of God (Romans 8:16). Wesley used this Scripture to explain the work the Spirit does in his children, arguing that the Spirit who inspired the Scriptures is also continuously at work confirming the experiential truths found in the text. In fact, Wesley believed that this inner witness of the Spirit confirmed what the Scriptures taught. He said: "What the Scripture promises, I enjoy. Come and see what Christianity has done here; and acknowledge it is of God."[7]

The Authority of the Word and the Spirit

Even though the early Methodists were accused of being enthusiasts, their enthusiasm was more than just emotional excess; it combined emotional engagement with reason and was anchored in a firm commitment to the authority of the Word and the Spirit. Howard Snyder points out the importance of this combination: "Renewal structure maintains an emphasis on the Spirit and Word as the basis of authority . . . if it veers to the right or the left at this point, it will become either a highly legalistic sect or an enthusiastic cult liable to extreme or heretical beliefs. In the case of Methodism, Wesley was able to maintain a balance which prevented either extreme."[8] Methodism sought to maintain a healthy balance of the Word and the Spirit, which contributed to the spiritual depth and lasting longevity of the movement.

Methodists were encouraged to immerse themselves in the Scriptures daily and to examine their lives according to the Bible. Wesley knew that regularly searching the Scriptures was necessary for a Christian to continue to grow in the faith. He was convinced that people encounter God experientially by reading, hearing, and meditating on the Bible. The more we learn about

God and his Word, the more we are able to know him personally. Though he wrote these words almost two centuries later, author and pastor A. W. Tozer summarizes this Wesleyan belief well: "The Bible is not an end in itself, but a means to bring men to an intimate and satisfying knowledge of God, that they may enter into Him, that they may delight in His Presence, may taste and know the inner sweetness of the very God Himself in the core and center of their hearts."[9]

The Bible isn't a question-and-answer book, but a resource through which we can learn about God's plan and purpose for our lives. Because the Bible provides this foundation for our faith, it ends up addressing many of life's toughest questions. Wesley placed a high emphasis on the importance of reading the Bible, and he repeatedly appealed to the Holy Scriptures as his doctrinal authority. He believed the "written word of God to be the only and sufficient rule both of Christian faith and practice."[10] In this, he was following the path forged by the Reformers, who taught and modeled a commitment to what they called *sola Scriptura*, the belief that the Bible is the final and normative authority on all matters it addresses. Wesley's passion for Scripture is best heard in his own passionate words: "O give me that book! At any price, give me the book of God! I have it: Here is knowledge enough for me. Let me be *homo unius libri* [a man of one book]."[11] In saying this, Wesley did not mean that other books were of no value to the Christian life, for he was an avid reader. He even compiled a fifty volume *Christian Library* for his people to read and study.[12] But Wesley understood that the Bible was unique among all other writings, the only true and authoritative record of God's revelation to us.

Wesley believed the Holy Spirit had inspired the Scriptures, and that the Holy Spirit is the one who gives us understanding of the Scriptures. He said, "The Spirit of God not only once inspired those who wrote it, but continually inspires, supernaturally assists, those who read it with earnest prayer."[13] Wesley believed that God speaks to us and inspires our understanding of the Bible through the inner working of the Spirit, something referred to as *dual inspiration*. The Holy Spirit *inspired* the ancient writers of the Scriptures and *inspires* contemporary readers today that they may comprehend the Word of God. This means there is a clear and ongoing need even now for the ongoing presence of the Holy Spirit as we engage in theological reflection and pursue understanding of the Scriptures. Without the assistance of the Holy Spirit, our reading of the Bible will be in vain.

Christians have always emphasized the importance of Scripture, believing there is a unique relationship between the Holy Spirit and the living Word of God. Unfortunately, some Christian groups have mistakenly placed a greater emphasis on one of these at the expense of the other. Wesley sought to model the integration of the two, believing that the dialectical balance of Spirit-Word was necessary, and that prayer is the primary medium that brings individuals into contact with the Spirit who inspired the original texts. Prayer enables us to hear what the Spirit of the Lord is saying through the Word of God.

I can remember the first time I sensed God speaking to me through his written Word. I was a new Christian reading my Bible, but I had no idea what I was doing. One night, I was sitting on my bed, reading through the book of Psalms, and when I read Psalm 51, the words on the page came to life. How? The words of the psalm, though written thousands of years ago, began to speak to me about the very situation I was facing at that moment. The prayer of David became my prayer. The words of the psalmist in verse 10, "Create in me a clean heart, O God, and renew a steadfast spirit within me," (NKJV) touched me deep within, and I felt God begin to melt my cold and stubborn heart. Since that night, I've continued to practice the discipline of reading the Bible regularly. Like Wesley, I want to encourage you to read God's Word for yourself and ask the Lord to speak to you from its pages.

The Empowering of the Holy Spirit

In addition to a focus on reading God's authoritative Word, the Methodist movement was marked by the empowering presence of the Holy Spirit working in the lives of men and women. Wesley believed that the revival he was seeing was a special work of the Holy Spirit for that time and place. He wrote, "It is plain to me that the whole work of God termed Methodism is an extraordinary dispensation of His providence."[14] For Wesley, the Spirit was not an abstract concept but a living reality, a person to be known and experienced. Wesley believed that being filled with the Spirit was the defining mark of "Scriptural Christianity," and in a sermon of the same title, which he preached at St. Mary's in Oxford on August 24, 1744, Wesley clearly emphasized the role of the Holy Spirit in the life of the Christian. He chose Acts 4:31 as his text: "And they were all filled with the Holy Ghost" (KJV). He made it clear that he was less concerned with the question of the extraordinary gifts of the Spirit (miracles, tongues, and healing, for example) and wanted to focus instead on the ordinary fruit that should accompany the life of a true Christian. He said, "Whether these gifts of the Holy Ghost were designed to remain in the Church throughout all ages, and whether or not they will be restored at the nearer approach of the "restitution of all things," are questions which it is not needful to decide. It was, therefore, for a more excellent purpose than this that "they were all filled with the Holy Ghost.""[15]

As the Methodist revival spread across England, the work of the Holy Spirit was becoming evident in the lives of thousands of believers, and Wesley became increasingly convinced that the empowering presence of the Spirit was one of the key signs or evidence of Scriptural Christianity. This was a significant shift in how many Christians thought about these things. Wesley was suggesting that true Christianity *must* be evidenced by outward signs of a changed or transformed life, that it was not simply a matter of affirming creeds or performing rituals. This sermon caused a bit of a scandal at Oxford and should remind us that Wesley's emphasis on "spiritual Christianity" was quite revolutionary at the time.[16] Wesley was affirming that being a Christian was more (but not less) than the affirmation of a confession or a creed; it was marked by a Spirit-filled life and clear signs of godliness in character and relationships.

Shortly after Wesley's Aldersgate experience, the early Methodist movement experienced the Holy Spirit during a prayer meeting in a powerful way. Along with others, John and Charles Wesley helped establish the Fetter Lane Society in May 1738, for the purpose of discipleship and accountability. During an all-night prayer meeting, the Holy Spirit showed up in a powerful way. John Wesley recorded the extraordinary encounter in his journal:

> Mr. Hall, Hinching, Ingham, Whitefield, Hutching, and my brother Charles were present at our love feast in Fetter Lane with about 60 of our brethren. About three in the morning, as we were continuing constant in prayer, the power of God came mightily upon us insomuch that many cried out for exceeding joy and many fell to the ground. As soon as we were recovered a little from that awe and amazement at the presence of His majesty, we broke out with one voice, "We praise Thee, O God, we acknowledge Thee to be the Lord."[17]

That Fetter Lane Society meeting marked a distinctive turning point in the early Methodist movement and is reminiscent of the description of the Day of Pentecost in the book of Acts, when the Holy Spirit fell upon those who were gathered together in prayer (Acts 1:8). In time the prayer meeting at Fetter Lane would come to be called the "Methodist Pentecost." Theologian Steve Seamands argues that Fetter Lane was a catalytic moment for Wesley and the Methodists:

> This outpouring of the Holy Spirit where, as Wesley says, "the power of God came mightily upon us," catapulted Wesley outward. It caused him and those gathered there to become other-directed as never before. Up until then Wesley had primarily been absorbed in his own quest for personal salvation. Aldersgate gave him the deep certainty he needed about that. However, as a result of the outpouring of the Holy Spirit at Fetter Lane, his focus shifted. Wesley was thrust out beyond himself so that the salvation of others, particularly those outside the church, became his burning passion.[18]

This event provides a glimpse into the fervent spirituality of the early Methodist movement, showing that these were people who were hungry for God to move in their lives. We cannot explain the explosive growth of the Wesleyan revival if we fail to understand the importance of the empowering presence of the Holy Spirit in the lives of individuals, and one of the outward signs of this was a fervent hunger for God, often expressed in prayer.

John Wesley wanted to see a revival of "true" Christianity, and this included the extraordinary or miraculous gifts of the Holy Spirit. He believed the gifts of the Spirit had waned after the time of Constantine, but he believed that they had never completely ceased. Wesley was convinced that the gifts of the Spirit had been intended to remain in the church throughout the ages. Randy Maddox wrote, "Since Wesley believed that his Methodist movement was recovering the holiness of the Early Church, it seems reasonable to suggest that he was open to renewed manifestation of even the extraordinary gifts among his followers."[19] In a lengthy letter to Conyers Middleton, Wesley argued that the miraculous gifts of the Spirit among the early church fathers were the attestation of their ministry and interpretation of Scripture. Wesley believed that the ancient church had a "standing power" to perform miracles which accompanied and attested to the truth of their proclamation of the gospel.[20]

Today there are godly men and women who have differing views concerning the miraculous gifts of the Spirit and the question of whether or not they continue to operate today. Cessationists believe that the "sign gifts" (tongues, prophecy, and healing) ceased with the time of the apostles, while charismatic Christians believe all the gifts of the Spirit are in continual operation and that believers possess and practice these spiritual gifts. [21] Regardless of where you fall on this issue, there is room for agreement that we should remain open to the Spirit's work in our lives. We cannot deny that it is the role and work of the Holy Spirit to give gifts to men and women in order to accomplish God's plans and purposes. We may disagree on which gifts are for today, but we should all agree that the Spirit continues to give gifts to God's people to use in his service.

This leads to the key question for us. Are we open to the work of the Holy Spirit in our churches? In our own lives? I believe we must be both open and discerning. I find that this balance is not easy to maintain, that many people are either open to the Spirit and not all that discerning, or they are discerning but not open, and in some cases, even resistant to the

Spirit's work. Perhaps the reason the Holy Spirit doesn't do more in our churches today is because we lack the fervent expectation and hunger found among the early Methodists. I would like to encourage you to pause and take a few minutes to reflect on your own experience of the person and work of the Holy Spirit. Is what you have been reading about in this chapter normal or abnormal in today's church?

PROFILE

William Seymour and the Rise of Pentecostalism

Pentecostalism is a modern-day movement that that can be traced to the Azusa Street Mission in Los Angeles, California in 1907. It began with a humble black minister named William Seymour who came under the influence of holiness teaching around 1900, while he was living in Cincinnati. In 1906, Seymour moved to Los Angeles and eventually started a prayer meeting in the home of Richard and Ruth Asberry at 214 Bonnie Brae Street. After months of prayer and fasting, Seymour and several others experienced being filled with the Holy Spirit. The prayer meeting soon outgrew the Asberrys' home, and they moved to an old, abandoned African Methodist Episcopal Church on Azusa Street. They cleaned up the building and began to hold services, and an amazing revival ensued.

Many people came to the meetings and were influenced

by the invitation to receive the baptism of the Holy Ghost. As word of what was happening at Azusa began to spread across the United States, men and women came from all over the country to experience the baptism of the Holy Spirit. From Azusa Street, the Pentecostal message spread around the world.

The Pentecostal movement has become the fastest-growing body of Christians in the world, at a rate of 13 million new believers a year, which amounts to around 35 thousand a day, and altogether there are nearly a half billion followers. Pentecostal believers are present in almost every denomination and every part of the world, including the Catholic and Orthodox churches. It is estimated that the Catholic Charismatic Renewal is currently present in more than two hundred countries and has touched the lives of over 160 thousand Catholics worldwide. The largest Protestant church in the world is a Pentecostal church in Korea called the Yoido Full Gospel Church, where over 240,000 people attend each week. Pentecostal spirituality is marked by an emphasis on a personal relationship with Jesus Christ, baptism in the Holy Spirit, divine healing and miracles, and missionary zeal.[22]

The Holy Spirit and You

As we draw near the close of this chapter and consider what we can learn for our own lives from the Wesleyan movement, I want to begin with a personal question: Have you had an encounter with the person and work of the Holy Spirit? By this I mean something that is as real as the sun shining on your face, the summer breeze blowing through your hair, or the sand in your toes. For some of you, it may seem crazy to consider the possibility of an encounter with God. But Wesley reminds us that this experience is available to us. You and I can experience the fullness of the Holy Spirit.

I say this not as a theologian or pastor, but as an ordinary guy whose life has been deeply touched and impacted by the Holy Spirit's work. Like everyone, I have had my fair share of struggles, doubts, and fears. When I became a believer, I was raw and rough around the edges. I needed the Lord to give me the strength and power to overcome my sinful desires, to resist my old lifestyle and the things that were contrary to my new life in Christ. I needed more than just knowledge of the truth, as important as that is. I needed to experience it for myself firsthand.

Then, one night, it happened. I had my first encounter with the Holy Spirit while I was attending a young adult retreat in the beautiful mountains of east Tennessee. As I prayed, I had an overwhelming sense of the Spirit's presence in my life. I could literally feel the Holy Spirit fill me from the top of my head to the toes of my feet. It was like an electric current shot through my whole body. This was not just a physical experience, but I felt my heart and mind renewed as well. I left that retreat changed, with a renewed sense that God was present with me, and that he would bring victory in my life. My life has continued to change since that night as I've grown in Christ, and I am still seeking to walk in the Spirit every day.

I believe the Holy Spirit is available for all Christians to experience today. The Spirit wants to bring each of us into a closer and more intimate relationship with Christ. You don't have to be super-spiritual to be open to the Spirit's influence in your life. There is a growing hunger among ordinary Christians who want to experience the Spirit in their own everyday lives. Today, because of this hunger, a fresh renewal of the Holy Spirit is taking place in churches, denominations, and networks of all kinds across the country and around the world. As you read the next few pages, I invite you to open your heart and mind to find out more about the person and work of the Spirit.

The Holy Spirit wants to use you more than you'll ever know. But even better, God wants you to know him, even as he knows you. We must learn to surrender our hearts and lives to him. As we conclude, I want to share several ways that you can be open to the Spirit in your everyday life.

1. THE SPIRIT WILL BE YOUR GUIDE

Many people have no sense of purpose or direction for their lives. They make decisions as though they're playing a game of chance, careless of the consequences, and their choices often lead to chaos and disorder. But a follower of Christ no longer needs to live this way. We are not left alone to figure things out on our own. The Bible is clear that God is with us and that the Holy Spirit wants to guide and direct us in everything that we do. Jesus said, "When He, the Spirit of truth, has come, He will guide you into all truth" (John 16:13 NKJV). The Spirit is given to us as a guide to lead us in the way we should live. It is God's deepest desire that we seek his wisdom and will in every area of our lives.

I regularly take time out of each day to ask the Holy Spirit to guide me. I begin by praying each morning, *Holy Spirit, lead and guide me today.* He will guide you, too, if you will ask and be open to his leading. God may not speak in an audible voice from heaven, but often he speaks as a quiet voice within. At times, his voice can be as faint as a whisper, and if we are not careful, we will miss it.

When you pray, take some time to stop and listen for God to respond. Many people treat prayer as a monologue rather than a dialogue. Don't just talk to God—pause and let him talk back to you. Be patient and listen. Are you seeking God's will for your life or facing an important life-changing decision? Trust the Lord and his Word to show you the answers to all of life's problems and challenges. Don't be afraid to ask God for direction. He speaks to those who are willing to ask and listen.

2. POWER TO BE A WITNESS

Many people are afraid to share their faith with others. I think when we are afraid to share, it's often because we fear what others will think or that they will reject us. The Bible says, "God has not given us a spirit of fear, but of power and of love and of a sound mind" (2 Timothy 1:7 NKJV). Here, then, is another way you can rely on the Holy Spirit. As you step out to share your faith with others, trust that the Holy Spirit will help you move past your fears and share with boldness.

At times, when we tell someone about Christ, we may rely on our own persuasiveness rather than seeking the power of the Holy Spirit. Instead, we need to ask the Spirit to fill us with his power so that we can be effective witnesses. Jesus promised, "You shall receive power when the Holy Spirit has come upon you; and you shall be witnesses to Me" (Acts 1:8 NKJV). Jesus promised us the power of the Spirit; all we have to do is ask for it. Pastor David Martyn Lloyd-Jones reminds us, "It is always right to seek the fullness of the Spirit—we are exhorted to do so."[23] Too many believers are weak in their faith and need the fullness of the Spirit in their lives. Don't be ashamed to ask for the Holy Spirit to give you the power to be a witness. In the book of Acts, the church prayed, "Grant to Your servants that with all boldness they may speak Your word," and when they finished praying, "they were all filled with the Holy Spirit, and they spoke the word of God with boldness" (Acts 4:29–31 NKJV). Ask the Lord for boldness, open your heart, and let the Holy Spirit give you power to be a witness for Christ today.

Conclusion

Hopefully this chapter has highlighted the work of the Holy Spirit in the growth and spread of the Wesleyan movement. And I hope you have seen that, in order for a revival movement to begin and to grow today as well, we need the Holy Spirit. The Spirit enables us and empowers us to live the Christian life, yet in many churches today, the Holy Spirit is rarely mentioned. The Spirit is neglected in many Christians' individual lives as well, as we attempt to do God's work in our own power and strength instead of relying on him. Many churches place their focus on maintaining buildings and planning budgets rather than seeking God's powerful presence through prayer. Consequently, churches across the country are essentially dying. They are desperately in need of spiritual renewal because they have lost the presence and power of the Holy Spirit. "Come, Holy Spirit!" is a prayer that hungry men and women have prayed for over two thousand years of church history.

If we scan the pages of church history, we can see that the Holy Spirit has always been present. At the very heart of the Methodist movement was a robust Spirit-filled faith rooted in the Word. The early Methodist movement had a balanced emphasis on personal experience that was sustained by spiritual practices called the means of grace (we will discuss these in detail in the next chapter), and as the movement spread, ordinary men and women went out in the power of the Spirit to share the gospel with others. If we want to see a movement in our day, we have to be willing to empower people to ministry and be open to the person and work of the Holy Spirit. Since so much of this chapter is personal, I want to end this chapter with a prayer.

> *Holy Spirit, I need you. I realize that I cannot make it without you in my life. Guide me in the way that I should go. Order my steps in your Word. Come and assist my prayer life. Empower me to be a witness for Jesus Christ. Help me share the message of faith in the power of your Spirit. Give me a holy boldness to speak your words. In the name of the Father, Son, and the Holy Spirit. Amen.*

CHAPTER 5

DISCIPLESHIP SYSTEMS

*The Wesleyan revolution is an illustration that
long-lasting spiritual transformation is not the
product of dynamic preaching . . . It comes only
through disciple building.*

D. MICHAEL HENDERSON

M any churches have a linear discipleship program, a one-
size-fits-all approach that attempts to funnel everyone
through the same process. Some churches simply use the latest
program or book the pastor has read in the hope that what was
successful for a large church across the country will also work
for them, even though it's a different geographical and social
context involving different people. My experience as a pastor
and church leader, however, has taught me that the process of

discipleship doesn't work this way. The system or process that works so well in California or New York may not yield the same results when you try it in Tennessee. While the means of grace are the same for all believers, the process of how you introduce people to Jesus, train them, and continue to support them in spiritual growth differs from place to place. You may need to study your own culture and context to learn how to effectively grow disciples right where you are.

Christianity began as an organic, grassroots movement over two thousand years ago. By organic, I mean that it was a movement that grew and developed in the manner of a living organism. The Bible uses various metaphors to describe the process of spiritual growth, many derived from farming and gardening. The Bible speaks of sowing and reaping (John 4:37; 2 Cor. 9:6), planting and watering (1 Cor. 3:6), growing (1 Pet. 2:2; 2 Pet. 3:18), and bearing fruit (Matt. 7:17–20; John 15:1–16; Gal. 5:22).

The Bible also uses metaphors related to human relationships and the human body to describe growth. The church is spoken of using relational pictures such as that of a family wherein we have brothers, sisters, mothers, and fathers. It's also referred to as the bride of Christ and as the body of Christ. In 1 Corinthians 12:12–27, Paul talks about the body as a distinct metaphor for Christ's church, and in Paul's body metaphor, every part has an important role to play in the whole.

It's significant to note that nowhere in the New Testament do we find the word "church" referring to a building. All references to the church denote a group of individuals who have gathered or assembled together in the name of Jesus Christ. The Greek word for church is *ecclesia*, which literally means "the called-out ones." But this nuance and much of the organic language describing the church has been lost in translation. Many English dictionaries describe a church as "a *place* of public worship," and over the centuries, the concept of church has shifted from a gathering of people to a building or a place. To recapture the movement dynamics present in the early church, which led to much of its growth, we must recover an organic—and biblical—understanding of what it means to *be* the church.

The church is the spiritual, living body of Christ. Like all healthy organisms, it requires numerous ecosystems that work together to enable it to fulfill its intended purpose and maintain overall health. An ecosystem is a community of living things that interact with each other, requiring continual change and adaptation. The church is no different. The capacity to change and adapt is a requirement for a healthy, growing church. As Leonard Sweet says, "We must develop ministries that continually adjust and change with our continually changing culture."[1] In a similar way, a church's discipleship strategy must be structured enough to maintain order, but organic enough to change with the ongoing needs of the church as it grows, or the church's growth will be hindered. An organic understanding of discipleship may necessitate a shift in thinking, a shift from existing systems and structures to new ones, ones more aligned with biblical terms and concepts. Organic discipleship is not a program or curriculum. It is about learning the natural rhythms of discipleship within your church context, the circumstances and relationships in which the Holy Spirit is working to bring life and growth.

One of the great lessons we are reminded of by the Wesleyan revival is that the purpose of the church is to make and multiply disciples. Perhaps more than anything, it was the *intentional* discipleship systems that contributed to the growth and longevity of the movement. One obvious reason so many churches struggle with making disciples is that they do not have a plan for it. In addition, many church leaders have not personally experienced what it is to live in healthy Christian community. Wesley reminds us that when these things are lost, the church must endeavor to rediscover the power of biblical discipleship and Christian community. As we will see, Wesley's discipleship ecosystem was intentional and flexible, moving people back and forth through three interlocking discipleship groups: societies, class meetings, and bands. Let's take a closer look at this ecosystem and what we can learn from it to apply to our own context today.

Break with the Moravians: Conflict and Contributions

Perhaps more than any other movement, we've seen that the Moravians made significant contributions to John Wesley's personal spiritual journey and to his understanding of discipleship. Two of the greatest contributions of the Moravians were in "clarifying and leading him into the experience of saving faith, and in providing him models of Christian life in community."[2] Yet Wesley had a slow and gradual falling out with the Moravians, beginning when he traveled to Herrnhut to visit them. He talked with their leader, Count Zinzendorf, and observed the lifestyle and religious practices of their community. At the time he was impressed with their unity and piety, yet just a few months after his return to England, Wesley became more critical of the community. He complained that they were too passive and did not exercise enough care in practicing spiritual disciplines, such as prayer, fasting, Communion, and Bible study. He also felt they overemphasized the internal witness of the Spirit and had made assurance a requirement for salvation. These differences were the beginnings of an eventual rift with the Moravians.

The break became apparent, spilling into the open, when they disagreed over the direction of the Fetter Lane Society. With Wesley traveling more and more to meet with people in the growing Methodist revival movement, the Fetter Lane Society increasingly came under the control of Moravian leaders. A struggle ensued between Wesley and the Moravian leader Phillip Molther, who taught a doctrine of stillness that was in direct opposition to Wesley's emphasis on the means of grace. Molther taught that people should abstain from all means of grace and simply "be still" until the Lord gave them true faith. Wesley, on the other hand, taught that the means of grace, including the sacraments, are also ways we encounter the Lord. The conflict came to a head in July of 1740 and Wesley and the Moravians parted ways, leaving control of Fetter Lane to the Moravian leaders. Wesley's two years of involvement at Fetter Lane was not a loss, however, as it allowed him to further develop his thinking about the important role of community and how to create discipleship groups conducive to ongoing spiritual growth.

Wesley the Master Organizer

Shortly after his break with the Moravians, Wesley began to fully implement his own ideas of discipleship among the growing Methodist movement. As Michael Henderson notes, "Some radical changes were about to take place in his life and which would give him the opportunity to develop his own instructional system and to control it completely."[3] The Foundry in London became the new epicenter for the Methodist movement. The Foundry had been an armory where cannons were made, but an explosion had destroyed most of the building. Wesley and his colleagues set out to repair the Foundry and turn it into the headquarters for the movement. They remodeled the old structure and built a chapel that could seat fifteen hundred people, a large room that would accommodate three hundred people, a book room to sell his books and pamphlets and tracts, a school for children, and a shelter for widows. It was at the Foundry that Wesley's ideas for the recovery of Scriptural Christianity began to gain some traction and spread.

Wesley had the mind of a master architect, and he was gifted to create an infrastructure to facilitate the growth and development of the movement. Wesley had an innate understanding of how faith is influenced by social environment. Malcolm Gladwell notes in *The Tipping Point* the significance of Wesley's disciple-making groups, highlighting his organizational genius and emphasis on community:

> He wasn't one person with ties to many other people. He was one person with ties to many groups, which is a small but critical distinction. Wesley realized that if you wanted to bring about a fundamental change in peoples' belief and behavior, a change that would persist and serve as an example to others, you needed to create a community around them, where those new beliefs could be practiced and expressed and nurtured.[4]

Wesley created a holistic disciple-making ecosystem that placed people in communities of vital relationships for ongoing spiritual growth. He understood that disciples are made in community, not in isolation, warning that "preaching like an apostle, without joining together those that are awakened and training them up in the ways of God, is only begetting children for the murderer."[5] Wesley knew a steady diet of preaching alone was not enough to keep people in the faith. He wrote, "I determined, by the grace of God, not to strike one stroke in any place where I cannot follow the blow."[6] Wesley followed the "blow" of salvation by putting people into groups to make sure they continued to grow in Christ.

What emerged at the Foundry was similar to some of Wesley's previous experiences with group discipleship in the Holy Club and the Moravian band meetings. He organized people into three interlocking discipleship groups called societies, class meetings, and bands. D. Michael Henderson explains some of the rationale for the different groups: "It could be said metaphorically that the society aimed for the head, the class meeting for the hands, and the band for the heart."[7] Let's break down the structure further by looking at each of the three individually while noting how each relates to the others in the overall system. [8]

SOCIETIES

The largest element of the discipleship ecosystem was the Methodist society. Over the years, the Wesleys had been involved with several "experimental" groups like the Fetter Lane Society. Religious societies were common in England at the time as they allowed people to gather together to pursue a deeper faith. Converts to the Methodist way wanted to meet with Wesley, and the society model provided a context for that to happen.

The society included a combination of existing, official members plus any others who were interested in Methodism. It was a place to bring friends or interested visitors and provided a gathering where people could connect beyond the field preaching and the invitation of a friend to learn more about the tenets of Methodism. It was a place of education that included times of preaching, lecturing, public reading, and hymn singing. Wesley himself described these societies in this way:

> This was the rise of the United Society, first at London and then in other places. Such a Society is no other than a company of [people] having the form and seeking the power of godliness, united in order to pray together, to receive the word of exhortation, and to watch over one another in love, that they may help each other to work out their salvation.[9]

Analogies are not always helpful, but I like to think of the Methodist society as a net designed to catch and retain a large number of people. The society held them all together and provided an important framework for the Methodist discipleship ecosystem. Averaging fifty or more people, societies provided a cognitive learning environment for the Methodists in a manner similar to our modern churches. Yet the society was merely a starting point for involvement. Those who attended the society were expected, and in most cases required, to join a class meeting if they wished to formally identify as a Methodist.

Wesley established dozens of these Methodists societies in cities like London, Bristol, and Newcastle to gather people with "only one condition previously required in those who desire admission into this society, a desire to flee from the wrath to come, and to be saved from their sins."[10] Each society was part of a much larger network of societies called the United Societies. From the beginning, Methodism was organized as a network of networks, perhaps similar to some of our church planting networks today. The leaders of each society were connected through this network approach, which offered relational support for them. Societies included all the Methodists in a given area or city, and the term "society" was used synonymously with the term "congregation." Eventually, these societies became churches when Methodism evolved into a formal denomination in North America after the Revolutionary War and in England after Methodism officially separated itself from the Church of England.

CLASS MEETINGS

One author describes the class meeting as the "keystone of the entire Methodist edifice."[11] By 1741, The Foundry Society had grown to over nine hundred members and other societies were growing similarly. As we will read about in the next section,

Wesley encouraged those who attended society meetings to be involved in smaller band meetings as well, a practice he had adopted from the Moravians. But these were not multiplying fast enough to keep up with the growing needs of the movement as new people joined. To keep things from falling apart, a third structure was needed to help fill the gap for the growing numbers. Almost by chance, the answer was found during a financial campaign to raise funds for the building of the New Room meeting space in Bristol and the remodeling of the Foundry. A sea captain named Foy suggested dividing the societies into smaller groups of twelve, each with a leader who would be responsible for collecting funds from the group and turning in twelve pence a week. These smaller groups were not the same as the bands, which met for encouragement and accountability in small groups. Wesley called these twelve-fold divisions of the society *classes,* taking the term from the Latin word *classis,* meaning "division."

The class meetings were essentially home churches that met weekly for prayer, instruction, and mutual fellowship. Because they were smaller, they were able to spread the movement into the neighborhoods where members lived. Those attending a class meeting often stayed together for years. Each class meeting had a designated class leader who provided spiritual oversight for the group, and Wesley described the duties of the class leader in this way:

> That it may the more easily be discerned, whether they are indeed working out their own salvation, each society is divided into small companies, called classes, according to their respective places of abode. There are about twelve persons in every class; one of whom is styled the Leader. It is his business: (1) To see each person in his class once a week at least, in order to inquire how their souls prosper; to

advise, reprove, comfort, or exhort, as occasion may require; to receive what they are willing to give toward the relief of the poor; (2) To meet the Minister and the Stewards of the society once a week; in order to inform the Minister of any that are sick, or of any that walk disorderly, and will not be reproved; to pay to the Stewards what they have received of their several classes in the week preceding; and to show their account of what each person has contributed.[12]

The class meeting was held once a week and included both men and women and people of all ages and social backgrounds. The meeting started promptly at the time designated and began with a hymn. The leader would then give a short testimony of the previous week's experiences and then each person in the group reported on his or her spiritual progress or needs and received prayer and support from the group. Wesley's instruction for the class meetings included admonishing Methodists to do the following things: first, do no harm and avoid evil; do good of every possible sort; and attend upon all the ordinances of God, including prayer, the sacraments, searching the Scriptures, and fasting. According to George Hunter, Wesley "was driven to multiplying 'classes' for these served best as recruiting groups, as ports of entry for new people, and for involving awakened people with the gospel and power."[13]

The class meeting soon became the backbone of the Methodist movement and was required for membership, which is vastly different from how many Christians today view church membership. Often, being a member of a church today consists of having your name on a membership roll or occasionally attending on Sunday morning. However, in the early Methodist movement, you could not call yourself a Methodist if you were not a member of a class meeting. Wesley even began issuing quarterly "tickets" to each class member, bearing the person's name, the date, a Scripture verse, and the signature of either Wesley or one of his leaders as proof of membership. This proof allowed them to attend the quarterly love feasts, which were a communal meal shared among Christians that recalled the meals Jesus shared with his disciples. I have a quarterly ticket from 1842 on my desk that belonged to a woman named Maria Snyder and was signed by her minister. It was a person's membership in the class meeting, not the society, that made one a Methodist.

In our own era of widespread church decline and lack of religious involvement, it may seem strange that people would submit themselves to such a high level of commitment. But Wesley knew that this was exactly what people were hungry for—a commitment. The early Methodists were men and women who were fully committed to being radical Christians, and thousands gladly gave their lives to the growing movement. D. Michael Henderson offers the following ten reasons why the class meeting was so successful:

It furnished an environment in which cognitive concepts could be experimentally or experientially tested.

It served as a purging or pruning instrument to the "dead wood" out of the society.

It was a training ground for leaders.

It was a point of entry capable of incorporating large numbers of new people quickly.

It financed the movement through penny collections.

Its accounting system provided constant and immediate record of the strengths and size of the movement.

It forced 100 percent mobilization and participation of the membership.

It gave every member a voice in the affairs of Methodism.

It allowed people to practice speaking their inner feelings.
It provided the milieu for resolving conflicts within the
society by immediate face-to-face confrontation.[14]

It was in these smaller, more intentional class meetings that
dynamic discipleship occurred. The class meeting eventually
became the point of entry into Methodism, and perhaps more
than any other innovation was what made Methodism multiply
and grow as quickly as it did. Commenting on the legacy of the
Methodist class meeting, the famous evangelist D. L. Moody
once said, "The Methodist class-meetings are the best institutions for training converts the world ever saw."[15] Methodists
themselves came to refer to the class meetings as the "soul" and
"sinews" of Methodism.

BANDS

While the societies were used to gather people in larger numbers
for teaching and edification, and the class meetings provided
space for more in-depth discipleship, Wesley knew that one
additional structure was still necessary. He called it the band
meeting, and he believed it provided the best potential for spiritual growth and development. The band was even smaller than
the class, a more intentional group with fewer members but more
rigorous requirements. The bands were divided by gender and
marital status, and they were designed to provide a forum where
the members of the group could confess their sins, then encourage and pray for one another. For many contemporary Christians,
the intimacy and accountability of the band meeting might seem
a little intense, even intrusive. According to Kevin Watson and
Scott T. Kisker, "The honesty and integrity of the bands is tre-
mendously rare in our culture, even within the contemporary
church. Through them God ministered sanctifying grace in

intimate space."[16] However, the band meeting was a place where many of the Methodist leaders were formed.

The rules of the band were as follows:

> The design of our meeting is to obey that command of
>   God, "Confess your faults to one another, and to pray
>   one for another, that ye may be healed" (James 5:16).
>   To this end, we intend:
> To meet once a week, at the least.
> To come punctually at the hour appointed, without some
>   extraordinary reason.
> To begin (those who are present) exactly at the hour, with
>   singing or prayer.
> To speak each of us in order, freely and plainly, the true
>   state of our souls, with the faults we have committed
>   in thought, word, or deed, and the temptations we
>   have felt since our last meeting.
> To end every meeting with prayer suited to the state of
>   each person present.
> To desire some person among us to speak his own state
>   first, and then to ask the rest, in order, as many and as
>   searching questions as may be, concerning their state,
>   sins, and temptations.[17]

This short account gives us a glimpse into what it was like to participate in one of the meetings. Wesley wanted the members of a band to show constant progress in their walk with the Lord, and through the grace of God, these groups provided structure and relationships that fostered this progress. Wesley exhorted them to:

> Never omit meeting your Class or Band; never absent your-
> self from any public meeting. These are the very sinews of

our Society; and whatever weakens or tends to weaken our regard for these, or our exactness in attending them, strikes at the very root of our community. As one saith, "That part of our economy, the private weekly meetings for prayer, examination, and particular exhortation, has been the greatest means of deepening and confirming every blessing that was received by the word preached, and of diffusing it to others, who could not attend the public ministry; whereas, without this religious connection and intercourse, the most ardent attempts, by mere preaching, have proved of no lasting uses."[18]

Methodist scholar Kevin Watson has co-authored a helpful book called *The Band Meeting: Rediscovering Relational Discipleship in Transformational Community*. In addition to sharing details about the structure and practices of Wesley's original band meetings, Kevin opens up about his own personal experience being involved in a band:

My first experience with a band meeting was the most profound experience of intimacy and vulnerability I had ever had up until that point. It was the first time I was invited that deeply into other men's lives. Being in that group helped me begin to tell the truth about my own life, especially the places where I was stuck in shame. It was not easy. But it was extremely powerful. That group exposed an unexamined lie I had believed: if anyone really knew me, they could never love me. In that band meeting, as we snuck off to an empty classroom to eat lunch together and confess sin, I began to risk letting people know me. By the grace of God, I discovered I was not alone. Someone else could know me as I was, and love me. And God's grace could bring lasting healing and transformation.[19]

After reading Kevin's account and hearing him share his story on stage at a recent conference, I felt a conviction that my own life lacked the depth of relationship Kevin was experiencing with others, so I made a decision to join a band myself. I began meeting with a group of men in my neighborhood. We come together each week to ask hard questions of each other and pray for one another. I am thankful God has put these men in my life and that I have a place where, every week, I can answer the question, "How is it with your soul?" I think the band meeting format can be adapted to any context. It doesn't take money or elaborate training, just three to five people who are willing to meet each week and ask deep spiritual questions. If you are interested in how bands would work in your context, I have included a contemporary model for the discipleship band meeting in the back of the book.

PROFILE

The Celtic Missionary Movement

When most of us think of Ireland, we think about green rolling hills and countryside covered in grass. Over one thousand years ago, on this little island, the world saw the birth of another influential movement—Celtic Christianity. Celtic Christianity stands out as one of the most vibrant and colorful Christian traditions the world has ever known.[20]

To understand Celtic Christianity, we can start by looking at the life and ministry of Saint Patrick, a person shrouded in mystery, superstition, and myth. While most of us are familiar with the holiday that bears his name and may know him as the man who drove the snakes out of Ireland and used the shamrock to explain the Trinity, we may not have heard the rest of the story. Patrick was the founding leader of the Celtic Christian church and was personally responsible for baptizing over a hundred thousand people, ordaining hundreds of priests, driving paganism from the shores of Ireland, and starting a movement in Ireland that helped preserve Christianity during the Middle Ages.

Patrick was born in 389 AD in a Christian home in Britain during a time when England was undefended by the Roman Empire. Irish raiders captured people in Britain and brought them back to Ireland as slaves. At the age of sixteen, Irish barbarians demolished Patrick's village and captured him. They brought him to the east coast of Ireland and sold him into slavery. During this time, Patrick spent many hours in prayer. Six years later, he escaped from his master and boarded a ship of traders who were heading to France. Eventually, he made his way back to Britain, where he had a vision and sensed a call to return to evangelize Ireland. Patrick immediately made plans to return to the land of his captivity.

Tradition has it that Patrick was appointed bishop and apostle to the Irish in 432. He traveled throughout the Irish countryside preaching the gospel. Paganism was the dominant religion at the time Patrick arrived, and he faced most of his opposition from the druids, men who were highly educated and practiced magic. They repeatedly attempted to kill Patrick, but God protected Patrick through a series of miracles.

As bishop of Ireland, Patrick was instrumental in the conversion of thousands of people, ordaining hundreds of clergy, and establishing churches and monasteries. Because of his ministry, Christianity spread through Ireland and into other parts of the British Isles. Patrick's mission alone was responsible for planting nearly seven hundred churches throughout Ireland, and the churches and monasteries he established became some of the most influential missionary centers in all of Europe.

Christianity spread throughout the British Isles under the gifted leadership of men such as Columba (521–597) who established monastic communities in Iona and Aidan in Lindsfarne. Contrary to stereotype, these monasteries did not house monastic recluses but served as discipleship training hubs commissioning missionaries to spread the gospel throughout Western Europe. It was these Irish monasteries that helped preserve the Christian faith when barbarian armies attacked and decimated cities in the collapsing remains of the Roman Empire.

Spiritual Practices

As the evangelical revival swept through England and North America, Wesley saw that many people fell away from the movement if they had no means to help them grow spiritually. Wesley knew that enthusiasm and experience were not enough. Neither was meeting together in small groups. Ordinary people also needed spiritual practices to help them grow in their faith, and these spiritual practices undergirded the Spirit-filled life.

For example, we know that Wesley was a man of prayer and regularly attended prayer meetings. He embodied what it means to live a prayerful life and later described a Methodist as one who, "prays without ceasing" and whose "heart is ever lifted up to God, at all times and in all places."[21] An associate of Wesley once remarked, "[Wesley] thought prayer to be more his business than anything else, and I have seen him come out of his closet with a serenity of face next to shining."[22] Wesley once said that prayer was the "grand means of drawing near to God," and he demonstrated his love for God by praying early in the morning, throughout the day, and late in the evening. Wesley encouraged and practiced private, public, and family prayer, and he believed that both private and corporate prayer were equally important. The Holy Spirit uses our prayers to draw us closer to God and to make us more like Jesus in thought, word, and deed.

The early church we read about in Acts was committed to many of these spiritual practices. We read in Acts 2:42 that they focused on "the apostles' teaching and to fellowship, to the breaking of bread and to prayer." John Wesley called these spiritual practices the "means of grace," meaning they are intentional practices or activities God uses to help Christians grow. Wesley believed the means of grace were "[an] outward sign, words, or actions, ordained of God, and appointed for this end, to be the ordinary channels whereby he might convey to men, preventing, justifying, or sanctifying grace."[23] Wesley felt that many of these God-given means had been lost or were no longer widely practiced and desperately needed to be recovered.

The means of grace include personal and corporate spiritual practices that promote spiritual growth in keeping with Paul's command to "discipline yourself for the purpose of godliness" (1 Tim. 4:7 NASB). The word Paul uses here, translated as "discipline," literally means "exercise," and it can be helpful to think of spiritual disciplines as exercises to strengthen us spiritually. Just as physical exercise promotes strength in the body, the spiritual practices promote godliness and growth in grace. They are vital to the individual and to the Christian community as we seek to become more like Christ.

There are many different means of grace available to us, but Wesley primarily emphasized three of them as the "chief" means. In a well-known sermon on the means of grace, he said: "The chief of these means are prayer, whether in secret or with the great congregation; searching the Scriptures; (which implies reading, hearing, and meditating thereon;) and receiving the Lord's supper, eating bread and drinking wine in remembrance of Him: And these we believe to be ordained of God, as the ordinary channels of conveying his grace to the souls of men."[24] In addition to these three, Wesley also emphasized fasting and public worship in much of his writing and speaking. As the wick of a candle needs wax to burn, so our spiritual life needs the means of grace to continue burning—or we risk burning out.

But discipleship doesn't just happen. Disciples must *intentionally* be committed to the ongoing practice of spiritual disciplines. Christian faith is more than a theory taught in a classroom or a set of ideas a person affirms; it is something a person practices in everyday life. Wesley believed discipleship should always be practical and applicable to real life. The spiritual disciplines are not for a select group of people living away from others or the exclusive domains of scholars but necessary for all Christians, from the pastor to the professor to the plumber. God has given us various spiritual practices to draw us closer to him and perfect holiness in our lives, but as was true in Wesley's day, many of these practices have been lost to the church today and desperately need to be recovered.

Can There Be Real Methodism without Class Meetings?

A few years ago, George Hunter had a conversation with a Dr. Byounghoon Kang, a Methodist pastor from South Korea, wherein he asked Dr. Kang what he thought about Methodism in America. Kang's reply was surprising: "From what I could tell, Methodism does not really exist in America." He continued, remarking that "your Methodist churches do not have class meetings, your people do not minister to each other through class meetings . . . In my church, and in most of our churches," he reported, "all of our people meet in class meetings. Our members' involvement in class meetings is even more important than their involvement in Sunday worship. Can there be real Methodism without class meetings?"[25]

While this is certainly a worthwhile question for Wesleyans and Methodists to consider, let me reframe Dr. Kang's question in broader terms that every Christian should consider: *Can there be real Christianity without discipleship in community?* Along with Wesley, I would argue that the answer is *no*.

Robby Gallaty is a pastor who has reappropriated Wesley's model for the contemporary church. In his book *Rediscovering Discipleship: Making Jesus' Final Words our First Work*, Robby shares how he is using the Wesleyan model to help train hundreds of leaders around the United States. Gallaty writes:

We have taken Wesley's model and created a Discipleship Pathway for believers to embark on: Congregation (Societies), Community (Classes), and Core (Bands). Members are asked to consider where they are in the pipeline of spiritual growth in order to take the next step of their journey. The Congregation (50+ people) is a weekly gathering, typically on Sunday morning. The purpose is to engage in a time of cele-bration through prayer, singing, study of Scriptures, and love for one another. The Community group (15–20 people), often a Bible study or small group, meets for behavioral change. The Core group, or D-Group, consists of gender specific groups of 3 to 5 for the purpose of commitment and accountability.[26]

Regardless of what you call it, Wesley's discipleship sys-tem of societies, class meetings, and band meetings offers us timeless principles useful for making disciples today. The Bible provides no evidence of a lone ranger in the body of Christ. Serious discipleship that grows people to spiritual maturity nec-essarily involves the whole body of Christ. Wesley recognized the importance of meeting together with other Christians to share our experiences, hold one another accountable, and pray for one another. The goal of the class meeting and the bands was to create a method and a means to help Christians grow in the faith and knowledge of the Lord Jesus Christ, and Wesley knew that growth wouldn't happen in isolation. We must constantly be growing in our relationship with the Lord, which requires interdependence with fellow believers.

Accountability, fellowship, encouragement, and study are only a few of the elements needed in these interdependent relationships. Wesley's basic ministry strategy was to meet the needs of the entire person through a discipleship ecosystem. A holistic approach will also move believers beyond themselves to reach out and meet the needs of others, both those in the larger "society" or congregation who are hurting and in need, as well as unbelievers in the broader community. Sadly, this type of holistic discipleship is missing in many churches today, yet they desperately need to be regained if we are going to sow a fresh revival movement in our day.

As we close this chapter, there may be some readers who are a little cautious and may think that Wesley's discipleship methods seem legalistic or too rigorous for modern sensibilities. Perhaps other readers have had a bad experience with an unhealthy controlling church or small group, or have heard of controlling communities that had negative effects on people's faith. I would argue that although this may be the case in some instances, it is more often the complete opposite. Most churches err on the side of not providing support for the discipleship journey. The church in much of the Western world is experiencing a discipleship crisis, and we are seeing the fallout from this deficiency with the drastic decline in churches and even whole denominations across the Western world.

The call to radical discipleship isn't just a Wesleyan or Methodist thing; it's a *Christian* thing. Plenty of non-Wesleyans have addressed the need to rediscover serious discipleship. At the First International Consultation on Discipleship, John Stott called attention to the "strange and disturbing paradox" of the contemporary Christian situation. He warned, "We have experienced enormous statistical growth without corresponding growth in discipleship. God is not pleased with superficial discipleship."[27] Sadly, some churches focus on evangelism at the expense of discipleship by seeking to win converts instead of making disciples, despite the fact that the goal of evangelism *is* disciple-making.

Alan Hirsch reminds us, "We can't make disciples based on a consumerist approach to the faith. We plainly cannot consume our way into discipleship . . . Consumption is detrimental to discipleship."[28] The result of consumerism on Christianity is what

Lutheran pastor Dietrich Bonhoeffer called "cheap grace" in his most famous work, *The Cost of Discipleship*, published in 1939. In *Growing True Disciples*, researcher George Barna reported that the church in America is comprised of "many converts, but shockingly few disciples."[29] What is the conclusion? We need to rediscover the lost art of disciple-making.

Wesley's discipleship systems not only made disciples, it produced leaders. With a high commitment to discipleship, thousands of leaders emerged out of the ranks of early Methodism. In the next chapter, we will meet some of the key leaders of the movement and learn how Wesley went about developing them.

CHAPTER 6

APOSTOLIC LEADERSHIP

*Not only did Wesley reach the masses; he made
leaders of thousands of them.*

HOWARD SNYDER

If you study the history of Christian movements, you will
begin to see that many of them are the result of a rediscovery, a return to a truth that was at the root of early Christian
belief and practice. Wesley saw the growing Methodist movement in this way, as a recovery movement in the long line of the
church tradition. Donald Thorsen points out that Wesley traced
the Methodist genealogy back to the "old religion," describing
Methodism as "the old religion, the religion of the Bible, the
religion of the primitive Church, the religion of the Church of
England."[1] For Wesley, Methodism was not something new and

innovative, but another link in an unbroken chain of true religion, a religion of the heart, which was "no other than love, the love of God and of all mankind."[2]

Methodism was both something old and something new. Wesley wanted to recover the old religion and connect his generation with the early church and its teachings, but Methodism was also something new, contextualized for his time and place, and Wesley was able to give old truth fresh expression. When he spoke about recovering "Scriptural Christianity" Wesley meant a return to the pure, undefiled "religion of the Bible, the religion of the primitive church."[3] This return to a more primitive form and practice of Christianity primarily meant returning to the spiritual vitality that was characteristic of the book of Acts and the early church. Wesley and the early Methodists had a vision to recapture a "contagious faith" and to spread it around the world: "Scriptural Christianity, as beginning to exist in individuals; as spreading from one to another; as covering the earth."[4]

The book of Acts reminds us that authentic Christianity rapidly reproduces. On the day of Pentecost, three thousand were added to the church, and they began to meet in home gatherings led by ordinary people (see Acts 2). Empowered by the Holy Spirit, God's people traveled and worked, taking the message and their faith in Jesus Christ with them. There was an apostolic DNA present in the early Christian movement, an impulse to share the message widely and multiply. As George Hunter III notes, this impulse was embraced by every believer. It's what we would call today a *lay movement*: "The identity of the church is located in its apostolic mission and ministry to people (and to the whole population) who are not yet people of faith, and this ministry and mission are primarily entrusted to the laity."[5] It was this vision of empowering ordinary, non-ordained people for God's mission that was at the heart of the Wesleyan revival.

All of God's people are empowered to do the work of ministry, whatever or wherever that may be.

Apostle means "one who is sent on a mission." In giving his disciples a commission to make disciples and preach the gospel, Jesus planted an apostolic impulse in the early Christian movement that was intended to extend the gospel into new territories and among new people groups. Alan Hirsch reminds us that this apostolic ministry is more of a function than an office. He describes it as "a pioneering function of the church, the capacity to extend Christianity as a healthy, integrated, innovative, reproducing movement, ever-expanding into new cultures."[6] The Wesleyan revival sought to recover this apostolic DNA by empowering the common people for the work of ministry, sending them out to share their faith, preach the gospel, and make disciples. Wesley's vision was clear: "Not to form any new sect; but to reform the nation, particularly the church; and to spread scriptural holiness over the land."[7]

Wesley's vision was to change the world by encouraging the people of God—every person who followed Jesus—to become "Scriptural Christians" and to live lives of vital faith and devotion to Christ. Theologians call this emphasis on the practical implications of our faith "practical theology," and in many ways John Wesley was a grassroots theologian, often developing his theology as he rode horseback from town to town. The doctrines of Methodism weren't compiled in academic volumes; they are present in the sermons and hymns of the movement. Wesley once said, "I design plain truth for plain people: Therefore, of set purpose, I abstain from all nice and philosophical speculations; from all perplexed and intricate reasonings; and, as far as possible, from even the show of learning, unless in sometimes citing the original Scriptures."[8] This does not mean Wesley was uninterested in doctrine and philosophy. After all, he was an Oxford-trained academic who understood the importance and necessity of good doctrine, having seen how the recovery of biblical doctrine had shaped the Reformation and led to the rise of Protestantism. But Wesley understood a simple truth: *doctrine without practice is not the faith of Christianity.* Wesley sought to always connect belief with practice in the hope that the Methodist movement would be marked by people living out what they claimed to believe.

The Tension of Tradition and Innovation

The Wesleyan synthesis could perhaps best be viewed as a tension between the embrace of tradition and the need for innovation. While Wesley was a traditional high church Anglican priest who honored church tradition, at the same time, he was an apostolic leader who was willing to innovate, willing to bring change to the structure and methods of the church in order to see the gospel shared and lives changed. His innovations often got him in trouble with Anglican church leaders. The Church of England taught and believed in the traditional "holy orders," a threefold order of ordained ministry they believed existed in continuity with the early church. It included the offices of bishop, priest, and deacon. These orders were called "holy" to indicate that they had been set apart for a special purpose. The word "order" designates an established pattern (from which we get the idea of ordination, a call to this order).

By the second century, the terms "bishop," "priest," and "deacon" had achieved widespread acceptance in forms that equated them with specific church offices, and these offices remained virtually unchanged in Wesley's day. The early church fathers had recognized all three offices and regarded them as essential to the church's structure. For example, the letters of Ignatius, bishop of

Antioch, defend the development of the threefold order of ordained ministry in his *Letter to the Magnesians*. [9] Along with several other Christian traditions, Anglicanism still holds to the historic three-fold order of the ordained ministry of bishops, priests, and deacons.

Yet while Wesley honored this tradition, he was far more concerned with saving souls, and he believed that the Lord was doing an extraordinary thing by raising up the Methodists and calling non-ordained men and women to preach and serve as leaders in the church. This, perhaps more than anything else, was why Wesley faced such opposition to his work. His embrace of non-ordained people to preach and lead bypassed the institutional hierarchy and upset the status quo. His empowerment of an army of non-ordained women and men was nothing short of revolutionary at a time when the church relied almost solely on clergy to accomplish Christ's mission.

Wesley worked to keep the old and the new in tension. He began to envision two kinds of ministerial orders: the ordinary Anglican clergy and the extraordinary Methodist preachers. Wesley saw a role for Anglican ministers in providing pastoral oversight of a congregation and administering the sacraments, while the purpose of the extraordinary Methodist preachers was preaching and evangelizing the lost. He makes this case in a sermon entitled "The Ministerial Office":

> So, the great High-Priest of our profession sent apostles and evangelists to proclaim glad tidings to all the world; and then Pastors, Preachers, and Teachers, to build up in the faith the congregations that should be found. But I do not find that ever the office of an Evangelist was the same with that of a Pastor, frequently called a Bishop. He presided over the flock, and administered the sacraments: The former assisted him, and preached the Word, either in one or more congregations.

I cannot prove from any part of the New Testament, or from any author of the three first centuries, that the office of an evangelist gave any man a right to act as a Pastor or Bishop. I believe these offices were considered as quite distinct from each other till the time of Constantine.[10]

Wesley used the Scriptures to aid him in embracing the tension he held between tradition and innovation, between the old and the new. He continued to believe in the need for the ordinary and established Anglican clergy, but he believed that there was an equally significant role for the non-ordained preachers and workers of the Methodist movement. The church was filled with ordained clergy, yet it was not meeting the need of the world to hear the gospel message. What was needed was an army of lay preachers and evangelists who would preach the good news at every highway and in the hedges. To this vision, Wesley was willing to give his life, dedicating his time and energy to empower a new and extraordinary order of ministry.

It's worth saying that Wesley was not the only innovator in church history. He was merely responding to the unique context in which he lived and addressing the vital needs of his day. In many ways, he was simply one Christian leader in a long line of innovators and reformers who challenged institutional excess and corruption that needed to be corrected. This list includes people like John Wycliffe, the great Bible translator; Martin Luther, who wrote the ninety-five theses to address church corruption; John Calvin, who brought reform to Geneva, and even Billy Graham, who challenged the status quo among modern evangelicals by working with Christians across denominational lines. Each one uniquely addressed a problem of his time, each one came under fire by the powers that be, yet each one helped to bring needed change and correction to the church.

Empowering Non-Ordained People

The rapid growth of Methodism would not have been possible without the sacrifices and dedication of the early Methodist leaders. Wesley famously wrote, "Give me one hundred preachers who fear nothing but sin and desire nothing but God, and I care not a straw whether they be clergymen or laymen, such alone will shake the gates of hell and set up the kingdom of heaven upon earth."[11] The leaders of early Methodism had grit and determination. They willingly gave their lives to the cause of Christ and the spread of Methodism. Among the early Methodist lay leaders were also prominent women of piety who led class meetings, visited the sick, and preached the gospel.

David Garrison, a pioneer in our understanding of church-planting movements, comments on this: "In church planting movements, the laity are clearly in the driver's seat. Unpaid, non-professional common men and women are leading the churches . . . Lay leadership is firmly grounded in the doctrine of the priesthood of the believer—the most egalitarian doctrine ever set forth."[12] As Garrison suggests, this recovery of "the priesthood of all believers"—an empowered laity—is the foundation for any successful multiplication movement. While it may seem unsurprising to find non-ordained, non-professional church leaders today, these changes were revolutionary shifts at the time of the Wesleyan revival.

Key Leaders of the Movements

As Wesley recruited new laity, several quickly rose to prominence within the movement as gifted, apostolic leaders. Wesley himself was an apostolic leader, one who had the ability to identify, train, and release other men and women. He had a God-given talent to recognize the best in people and to develop their leadership qualities. Many of these leaders helped Wesley spread the cause of Methodism throughout the British Isles, into North America, and eventually throughout the world. Each had a unique role and contributed in a special way to the spread of Methodism. Without them, the Methodist story would be incomplete.

CHARLES WESLEY

Wesley's younger brother, Charles, was his lifelong companion in ministry and a co-leader in the Methodist movement. Charles was a gifted preacher and songwriter, the author of over nine thousand hymns and poems, many of which can be found in the *Collection of Hymns for the Use of the People Called Methodist.* Several of these beloved hymns are well-known and instantly recognizable, including, "Hark! The Herald Angels Sing," "Love Divine," "Jesus, Lover of My Soul," and "O, For a Thousand Tongues." Many of his hymns are still sung in churches today.

From the very beginning, Wesley and Charles seemed to be well-suited for ministry together, each one bringing unique gifts and abilities to the ministry. The brothers were together from the earliest days of the movement and throughout its development. Both were ordained in the Church of England around the same time, they traveled together as missionaries to Georgia in the American colonies, and when they returned to England, both had an awakening experience. Wesley relied on Charles for personal counsel and assistance.

ADAM CLARKE

Adam Clarke was an Irishman who converted to Methodism in 1778 under the preaching of Thomas Barber. Clarke was a teenager when he dedicated his life to God, and at Wesley's invitation, he trained for the ministry. He was one of the first lay preachers ordained by Wesley, and he quickly rose to prominence in the Methodist movement. A gifted leader and preacher, a competent biblical scholar, and a prolific writer, Clarke had no formal university education, but he was fluent in at least twenty languages, including Greek, Latin, Hebrew, Samaritan, Syriac, Arabic, Persian, and Coptic.

By some estimates, Clarke preached over fifteen thousand sermons during his lifetime, speaking to the masses and writing books for the learned. Among his works is an eight-volume series called *Commentary on the Holy Scriptures*, which became required reading for Methodist clergy even long after his death. Clarke was beloved among Methodist preachers, and he served an impressive three-term presidency with the Wesleyan Conference. His writings contributed greatly to the spread of Wesley's doctrine of holiness. Though he died in 1832 of cholera, he left a lasting legacy that would continue to impact the development of Methodism for generations to come.

THOMAS COKE

Dr. Thomas Coke was a passionate soul-winner who joined the Methodist movement in 1772, two years after he was ordained in the Church of England. Within a year of his ordination, he was dismissed from the Anglican church because he had begun preaching like a Methodist. He joined the Methodist movement full-time, becoming one of Wesley's most able leaders and closest associates. Wesley designated him a co-superintendent, along with Francis Asbury, tasked with setting the fledging American Methodist Church in order, but he did not remain in that position for long.

Coke remained in America for a few years, but his heart was for the mission field. In 1789, he was appointed the head of the

Irish Conference, and for the rest of his life he was dedicated to supporting and promoting world missions. In his later years, he was especially passionate in his desire to bring the gospel to India, saying, "I am dead to Europe and alive for India." In 1814, he had an opportunity to take the gospel to Ceylon and India, but he died while engaged in prayer on his way to India. Today Dr. Coke is remembered as one of Wesley's greatest leaders and a champion for world missions.

FRANCIS ASBURY

The ministry of Francis Asbury is largely responsible for the growth of Methodism in America after the Revolutionary War. John Wesley sent Asbury to America to promote Methodism in the colonies, and soon after his arrival he became one of the primary leaders of the American movement. Although Asbury was English by birth, he won the hearts and souls of the American people. Throughout his forty-five-year ministry in America, he traveled nearly 300,000 miles on horseback, preached around 16,500 sermons, and ordained more than 4,000 preachers. He crossed the Allegheny Mountains sixty times, and for many years he visited nearly every colony at least once annually. His constant travels made him one of America's most recognizable figures. John Wigger, commenting on his popularity at the time, said, "He was more widely recognized face to face than any other person of his generation, including such national figures as Thomas Jefferson and George Washington."[13]

Asbury was a man of great piety and learning, and many remember him as a great man of prayer as well. Even in his constant travels and engagement in ministry, he still found time to pray. He was known to rise at four o'clock in the morning and spend two hours in prayer and meditation, and to pause seven times during the day to pray. He was a tireless leader who devoted his entire life to the call of Christ in America.

Although he dropped out of school before he was twelve years old, Asbury taught himself to read Latin, Greek, and Hebrew. He cultivated the love for learning among others, founding five schools and promoting Sunday school in churches to teach reading and writing to children. He read widely on various subjects of his day, often reading books while riding on horseback from place to place, a common practice of many Methodist circuit riders. Some have said that he was one of the most well-informed men of his day, able to converse on any subject.

Like Wesley, Asbury was a master at organizational leadership. He created something called a "district," a circuit of churches that preachers would serve on a rotating basis. In the early days of American Methodism, a "circuit rider" would travel from church to church to preach and minister. This enabled churches to exist where previously they had not been able to. Circuit Riders like Asbury braved the rigors of the frontier and were occasionally attacked by Native Americans. Several faced severe illness caused by constant exposure to the elements of nature. Although Asbury was plagued by bad health for much of his life, he continued his travels, even if it meant tying himself to his saddle to keep from falling from his horse. One story has it that he was once trailed by wolves, who followed him, waiting for him to fall and die. Asbury is sometimes referred to as the "American Bishop" of the Methodist movement.

WOMEN LEADERS

In addition to these men, there were several women who also became leaders in the Methodist revival. Although most leadership roles in the church were closed to women, Wesley and early Methodism were far ahead of their time in recognizing the gifts of women and allowing them to actively participate in Christian ministry. Women served at several different levels in the movement. Many of the class and band leaders were women, some of whom were engaged in preaching and leading souls to Christ. Wesley took note that God was using women in this manner and encouraged it, offering them training and teaching. Women such as Sarah Crosby, Mary Bosanquet, Hannah Harrison, Grace Murray, and Hester Ann Roe Rogers were among the prominent, non-ordained ministers of Methodism. They were examples of piety, learning, and leadership.

Mary Bosanquet became Methodism's first female preacher. She was a lay theologian of sorts and wrote a letter to John Wesley defending the right of women to preach the gospel. In her letter she argued that the Bible contained many accounts of women who were called by God to minister. In part due to her letter, Wesley began recognizing and affirming the extraordinary call of God on certain women to preach. In response to Mary Bosanquet's letter he wrote:

> I think that the strength of the cause rests thereon your having an *extraordinary* call. So I am persuaded has every one of our lay preachers; otherwise I could not countenance his preaching at all. It is plain to me that the whole work of God termed Methodism is an *extraordinary dispensation* of His providence. Therefore I do not wonder if several things occur therein which do not fall under the ordinary rules of discipline.[14]

In 1787, despite opposition by some male preachers, Wesley authorized Sarah Mallet to preach as well, so long as she agreed to keep Methodist doctrine and discipline. This was a bold stride toward the full recognition of women as preachers, which would not come about until long after Wesley's death. But we should not ignore how Wesley's own views on women in ministry were revolutionary in his day, and indeed, remain so today. Wesley believed that women had equal rights to the same positions and opportunities that men did. In a sermon entitled "On Visiting the Sick," he directly addressed the equal rights of women, saying:

> Let all you that have in your power assert the right which the God of nature has given you. Yield not to that bondage any longer! You, as well as men, are rational creatures. You, like them, were made in the image of God; you are equally candidates for immortality; you too are called of God, as you have time, to 'do good unto all men.'[15]

It's important to note that the rapid growth of Methodism would not have been possible without the tireless work and self-sacrifice of these early female Methodist leaders. Many of them gave their lives for the cause of Christ and to the spread of Methodism. If we look throughout the centuries, we will find that women contributed to the ministry of the church in significant ways, even though their involvement has rarely been free from controversy. Even today, many churches and denominations are still debating the role of women in the church. Some churches ordain women, while others do not. When it comes to the ordination of women, I believe that Christians should agree to disagree and choose to walk together in love despite differences of opinion. As an advocate for women's ordination myself, I think this provides for a healthy balance where people on both sides of the argument can be a part of the same church and serve a common mission.[16]

WESLEY'S 12 RULES
FOR LEADERS

1. Be diligent, never be unemployed a moment, never be triflingly employed, never while away time, spend no more time at any place than is strictly necessary.

2. Be serious. Let your motto be, 'Holiness unto the Lord.' Avoid all lightness as you would hell-fire, and laughing as you would cursing and swearing.

3. Touch no woman. Be as loving as you will, but hold your hands off 'em. Custom is nothing to us.

4. Believe evil of no one. If you see it done, well, else take heed how you credit it. Put the best construction on everything. You know the judge is always supposed to be on the prisoner's side.

5. Speak evil of no one, else your word especially would eat as doth a canker. Keep your thoughts within your own breast till you come to the person concerned.

6. Tell everyone what you think wrong in him, and that plainly, and as soon as may be, else it will fester in your own heart. Make all haste, therefore, to cast the fire out of your bosom.

7. Do nothing as a gentleman: you have no more to do with this character than with that of a dancing master. You are the servant of all, therefore . . .

8. Be ashamed of nothing but sin: not of fetching wood, or drawing water, if time permit; not of cleaning your own shoes or your neighbour's.

9. Take no money of any one. If they give you food when you are hungry, or clothes when you need them, it is

good. But not silver or gold. Let there be no pretence to say, "we grow rich by the Gospel."

10. Contract no debt without my knowledge.

11. Be punctual: do everything exactly at the time; and in general do not mend our rules, but keep them, not for wrath but for conscience sake.

12. Act in all things, not according to your own will, but as a son in the Gospel. As such, it is your part to employ your time in the manner which we direct: partly in visiting the flock from house to house (the sick in particular); partly, in such course of reading, meditation, and prayer, as we advise from time to time. Above all, if you labour with us in our Lord's vineyard, it is needful you should do that part of the work which we prescribe at those times and places which we judge most for His glory.[17]

Lessons from Wesley's Leadership

As we have already noted, John Wesley was a master organizational leader. With George Hunter, I would affirm that "The day for John Wesley's strategic wisdom is not over, for many of his principles have perennial validity. As Wesley the 'strategic genius' is rediscovered, he will become one of the strategic fountainheads of the Christian movement facing the twenty-first century."[18] As we conclude this chapter, I'd like to offer a few personal reflections on Wesley's leadership genius and how they apply to disciple-makers and church leaders everywhere.

FIRST, MODEL THE WAY THROUGH
YOUR OWN LEADERSHIP.

One reason Wesley had such a lasting impact on his followers is that he embodied what he taught and called others to—a radical commitment to Christ and the Methodist cause. He modeled this by his lifestyle, which matched his preaching. Steve Addison notes: "Wesley was able to inspire commitment to the Methodist cause because he embodied that commitment."[19] He was a true leader of the people, traveling thousands of miles on horseback, preaching and teaching the masses, yet still finding time to regularly meet with leaders across the country. They saw how he lived out his faith in the real world. For Wesley, there was no distinction between a private and a public faith. He walked with his leaders, he prayed with them, he fed the poor among them. He lived the life he sought to reproduce in others.

As leaders, it is important that we practice what we preach, because the people we are training will look at how we live and follow our example. As important as it is to preach the gospel, we must also practice it daily. Wesley knew that a leader's personal walk with God is one of the most important factors in his or her ability to develop godly leaders. We will reproduce what we are, and the most powerful message preached is a life on fire for God. So make sure the life you are living is one worthy for others to follow. Although none of us are perfect, we should strive to be present in the lives of the people we are seeking to develop, modeling the way through our lives and leadership.

Practically, we should look for ways to schedule time with the people we want to disciple outside of normal church functions. This time can include times of play, prayer, and sharing meals together. As with any worthwhile investment, discipleship will cost you something. It will take a sacrifice of time, energy, and emotion for the sake of others. I believe this is one of the reasons why discipleship does not happen very much in churches today. The cost is high. But this is a price we must pay if we are going to build healthy and thriving churches that serve the Lord faithfully.

SECOND, BEGIN TO DEVELOP A LEADERSHIP PIPELINE.

A leadership pipeline is an intentional system or structure that trains and equips people to become leaders. Wesley developed his leadership pipeline beginning with an individual attending class meetings and gradually progressing to the highest levels of leadership in the Methodist movement. The class meeting was where it all began, as that was where an individual's gifts were identified and began to be used in ministry to others. If a person was faithful to serve others in the class meeting, they continued on their way through the pipeline, eventually becoming a leader of their own class meeting. Wesley was constantly identifying, training, and appointing leaders who showed giftedness for ministry and were faithful in the work of preaching, teaching, evangelism, or helping with administration and the stewardship of finances. Wesley also appointed indigenous leaders who were raised up in local community. Who better to minister over a class meeting than a member of that community?

The early Methodist leaders were men and women of piety, and as Wesley empowered non-ordained leaders, the movement continued to multiply, growing rapidly throughout England. Wesley chose his leaders carefully, hand-picking them according to the gifts they demonstrated. He took his time and was quite serious about this. In a similar way, we must learn to be selective in whom we choose to disciple. We should look for people who are faithful, willing, and able to progress and grow in their discipleship. Discipleship does not require earning a degree or a Bible college education; it simply requires obedience and an investment of time and energy. Often, the leaders we need are ordinary men and women—including people who are already in our churches. One of the best places to find new leaders is to look at the faithful women and men leading your church small groups. We should seek to find men and women who have a passion and a hunger for Christ, because willingness to answer the call to follow Jesus is the only requirement to be a disciple of Jesus.

As a contemporary example of a leadership pipeline, one that resembles Wesley's own method of raising up leaders, I've learned a great deal from the work of Sea Coast Church in Mount Pleasant, South Carolina. Pastor Greg Surratt says, "Most of our pastors come from high-producing volunteers."[20] In order to provide maximum development and empowerment to its volunteers, Sea Coast has created its own leadership pipeline. Like Wesley's pipeline, the process begins with involvement in a small group. If faithful, a group member can go on to become a small group leader, rising to the level of small group coach to other small group leaders. Growth continues, leading to a transition from being a small group coach to becoming a ministry leader, until a person becomes a licensed minister and, eventually, a pastor. For more details on the Seacoast Leadership Pipeline, be sure to check out Appendix A.

THIRD, EMPOWER OTHERS ACCORDING TO THEIR GIFTS.

Wesley knew that everyone has different gifts, and that such gifts have been given for different works of ministry. He would ask of those who came to him, wanting to preach, "Have they the gifts (as well as the grace) for the work?" Upon reflection and after consulting with others, he sought to assign leaders to serve according to their giftedness. The Methodist structure was designed to allow people with different gifts to use those gifts at the appropriate place in the organization. D. Michael Henderson notes that "instead of trying to produce leaders, the Methodist system allowed the natural ability of its entire population to rise to its highest potential."[21] Wesley developed his followers by delegating ministry responsibilities to those who showed a passion for ministry, and if they were successful with the work given, they were entrusted with even more responsibility. Eventually he would send them out, giving them ministry responsibilities with greater challenges where failure was a real possibility. He believed that hands-on experience was the key to leadership growth, and it was a vital part of his discipleship curriculum.

Sadly, some church leaders today are either afraid or unwilling to give people significant roles with significant responsibility. Others fail to provide opportunities for service on a regular basis. It is possible for a leader training for pastoral ministry to spend years in classrooms attending college and seminary, only to graduate with little, if any, real ministry involvement. The church today needs to rethink how it structures ministry around mission and how to best delegate and empower people according to their gifts. Is it any wonder our discipleship is often anemic? Many followers of Christ today still believe it is the job of the pastor to do everything in the church. We must never neglect the importance of involving and empowering lay people in ministry.

FOURTH, UNDERSTAND THE NEED TO PROVIDE ONGOING SUPPORT.

Wesley never appointed people to a task without providing some type of ongoing support and supervision. He supervised his leaders and created structures for them to report on the state of their faith and their ministries. This gave his leaders an opportunity to reflect and review their ministry progress. He offered additional support by providing opportunities for local preachers and leaders to meet together annually and mutually encourage one another.

Supervision and support are essential components of leadership development, especially when training new believers. As important as it is to delegate the work and empower people to act, we must also be available to supervise and support them, making sure they stay on track. Without proper supervision, a new leader can easily crash and burn at the first failure. Supervision is an art that requires balancing the tension between micromanagement (watching too closely and failing to empower and release them) and a lack of supervision (not being available when there are questions or help is needed).

Conclusion

In this chapter we have seen that Methodism spread as non-ordained leaders were called, trained, and released to provide leadership. This emphasis on lay leadership spurred the rapid growth of the Methodist movement. Wesley identified and called out apostolic leaders who provided guidance to the growth of the movement and reached thousands of people for Christ. This included both men and women, a revolutionary shift away from the status quo.

While there is much we can learn from Wesley and his leadership, perhaps the most important takeaway is the passion they shared for the advancement of the kingdom of God. Dr. Robert Coleman is the author of *Nothing to Do but to Save Souls: John Wesley's Charge to His Preachers*, and I'd like to end this chapter with a challenge from this book, a word that is appropriate for church leaders today:

> It is my hope that looking again at the roots of Wesleyan evangelism, though it be but a brief glimpse, will bring us to see anew that deep conviction of truth which drove our forefathers to proclaim the Gospel and invite "whosoever will" to come to Christ. I think that all of us could well afford to spend some time reviewing the values that thrust us forth in ministry.[22]

CHAPTER 7

ORGANIC MULTIPLICATION

This revival of religion has spread to such a degree, as neither we nor our fathers had known. How extensive has it been! There is scarce a considerable town in the kingdom, where some have not been made witnesses of it.
JOHN WESLEY

Have you ever blown on a dandelion head and watched as the seeds floated away? As beautiful as those white fluffs appear, dancing in the wind, we should not be fooled to think they are disappearing from sight. Those white seeds have one mission in life: to multiply and to increase my frustration. This year, due to an overly rainy spring season, my yard was overtaken by a horde of dandelions. It required planning and hard work to defeat those yellow weeds, because dandelions are very good at what they are made to do. A single dandelion is capable of producing enough seeds to cover your entire lawn!

Nature can teach us many things about the way the kingdom of God operates, and one of those lessons is that all healthy, living things will naturally reproduce and multiply. Multiplication is the goal of every living thing, and we see this truth confirmed throughout the pages of the Bible. God created humankind, animals, and plants to reproduce. He told Adam and Eve to "be fruitful and multiply" (Gen. 1:28 NKJV). Reproduction is inherent in much of the agricultural language Jesus uses when he teaches and preaches. He used metaphors from nature and farming to teach his disciples lessons about the kingdom of God, and expected his disciples to reproduce what he had impressed upon them in the lives of others. Jesus imparted his message and his mission to his disciples so they would reproduce themselves, essentially, and make disciples of all nations. This reproductive DNA is one reason the early Christian community of several hundred people turned into a worldwide movement. Starting with twelve disciples, Christianity now claims over 2.1 billion members.

But how did we get there? In John 15:1–17, Jesus introduces us to the metaphor of the grapevine and its branches. He explains that the purpose of the vine (which represents Jesus) and the branches (which represent us, his followers) is to bear fruit. In other teachings, Jesus makes it clear that Christians are to work for and expect a harvest (Matt. 9:37–38; Luke 10:2). In other words, there are clear parallels between the work of farming or gardening and the work of ministry. In both cases, we should work in such a way that leads to the expected result: good fruit!

If we apply this analogy to the church today, it is a stark reminder that the church was never intended to be an end in and of itself. Rather, the purpose of the church is to reproduce, to bear fruit (disciples) and fulfill the Great Commission. Churches are dynamic and alive, full of excitement and energy, whenever they are reproducing and giving birth to new disciples and multiplying new churches. Why? Because in doing so, they are fulfilling their God-given purpose. In the Western church today, we desperately need to recover this biblical vision and find ways to once again become a reproducing, disciple-making movement. As we will see in this chapter, the Wesleyan revival is an excellent example of this. We will look at Wesley's legacy, especially how the movement spread into North America, and we'll draw some lessons on multiplication that are applicable for the church today.

Wesley's Final Years

Perhaps you've heard it said that wine gets better with age. I believe the same could be said of John Wesley, because he seemed to be most productive in his later years as the leader of the Methodist revival. One of the marks of an effective leader is his ability to prepare an organization to outlast his own leadership. Wesley understood this, and he worked hard to create an organizational structure and a leadership team that would continue to thrive long after his death. Instead of stepping back to retire, Wesley's final years were a time of great productivity in which he worked harder than ever to consolidate the movement.

There were several major developments in these latter years that assured the movement would continue. By the late 1770s, the Foundry, which had served as the headquarters of the movement in London, had become too small to hold ongoing gatherings, and there was a growing need to find new, permanent headquarters for Methodism. Out of this necessity, Wesley built what is now known as "Wesley Chapel" on City Road, which became the new center for the movement. In April 1777, he laid the foundation for the chapel on City Road, and Samuel Tooth, a class leader and local preacher, oversaw the work of building it. Far more than just a preaching house, it was the first Methodist chapel to include an altar and a communion rail, and it seated about fifteen hundred people. The chapel provided a much-needed home for Wesley and the other preachers, including their families and servants. After the foundation was laid, Wesley preached a sermon highlighting the rise of Methodism and connecting it to the "primitive religion" of the Bible. Some have called the chapel the "Mother of World Methodism" because it became the center for Methodist leadership, influence, and activities throughout the world.

As the movement expanded, the number of Methodist preachers continued to grow, and there was a need to organize them. In 1744, Wesley began meeting annually with his preachers to discuss Methodist doctrine and discipline and to appoint preachers to various locations for the coming year. This annual meeting became the forerunner for the Methodist Conference as we know it today. The conference gave new leaders a voice in the growing movement, and it strengthened their support of Wesley's leadership by connecting them to him personally. It gave these new leaders a sense of ownership over the movement and their own ministries. Although only a few attended the first conference, by the time of Wesley's death attendance numbered in the hundreds.

Although Methodism continued to grow and flourish throughout the British Isles, it wasn't long before it jumped beyond the borders of England, spreading to Ireland. Then, in 1760, Robert Strawbridge and his wife Elizabeth moved from

Ireland to America and became the first Methodist pioneers in the New World. Strawbridge established the first organized Methodist society and meetinghouse near Baltimore, Maryland, and under Strawbridge's ministry, John Evans became the first Methodist convert in America.

Soon after this, in 1766, Philip Embury and Barbara Heck (who were cousins and Irish Methodists), formed a Methodist class in New York City. Embury had converted under Wesley's ministry and become a non-ordained preacher in Ireland. Having seen the need for a society in New York, Heck convinced Embury to begin preaching again. Though only six people attended his first meeting, it soon grew into a large meetinghouse named the Upper Room.

Three years later, in 1769, Wesley sent two men, Richard Boardman and Joseph Pilmore, to serve as his assistants in America in response to a letter from a man named Thomas Taylor asking for "an able, experienced preacher." Two years later, Wesley sent two more preachers—Richard Wright and Francis Asbury—to assist in the work. In 1773, another two preachers were sent: Thomas Rankin and George Shadford.

Then, in 1778, Wesley made provisions for a stable governmental system that would all but assure the movement would remain intact after his death. On February 28, 1787, he composed the Deed of Declaration, giving legal rights to the preachers of the Methodist Conference. The deed listed one hundred preachers by name and gave them the right to meet once a year to elect a president and a secretary, to appoint preachers to circuits, to admit candidates for ministry, and to conduct general business for the Methodist Conference. The annual conference was also an opportunity for preachers to be heard, have fellowship with one another, and share their triumphs and trials from the previous year.

Some of the preachers who were not among the initial one hundred were initially offended that they had not been included in the meeting. In response, Wesley argued that all preachers could not attend because that would leave vacancies in many of the circuits. After Wesley's death, however, the conference extended the privileges of the Deed of Declaration to all preachers who were in full fellowship with the conference. The Deed of Declaration provided a lasting structure and foundation to the Methodist movement by granting the legal power of the church to its preachers. Even today, the Methodist Conference still meets every year, following many of the patterns and precedents first established by Wesley.

In the early years of Methodist missionary activity in the American colonies, non-ordained ministers were not allowed to administer the sacraments. This made the Methodists in America dependent upon the Anglican clergy to baptize their children and serve the Lord's Supper. Lay ministers like Strawbridge, however, felt it necessary to administer the sacraments—even though they were not officially ordained. It was because of this growing pressure to provide proper spiritual care for his flock in America that Wesley reluctantly decided to begin ordaining lay preachers for the work in America.

On September 18, 1784, Wesley ordained Richard Whatcoat and Thomas Vasey and dedicated Thomas Coke, who was already an Anglican priest. Coke and the two other men were sent to the Colonies with instructions for organizing the American Methodist Church, which included instructions for ordaining other ministers. There were also directions provided to install Coke and Francis Asbury as superintendents of the new church. Whatcoat and Vasey brought with them a prayer book based on the Anglican liturgy titled *The Sunday Service of the Methodists in North America.* They also brought a book of songs called *A*

Collection of Psalms and Hymns for the Lord's Day. The Sunday Service included a set of twenty-four doctrinal statements called the *"Articles of Religion,"* which were a simplified version of the Anglican Church's thirty-nine *Articles of Religion.*

On December 24, 1784, the American Methodists held the now-famous Christmas Conference at the Lovely Lane Chapel in Baltimore, Maryland. This meeting led to the organization of an entirely new church: The Methodist Episcopal Church in America. Asbury and Coke were unanimously re-elected as superintendents by the preachers gathered, and several preachers received ordination, permitting them to administer the sacraments. The newly formed church also added an article to its records recognizing the United States of America as a sovereign and independent nation. The conference attendees approved a motion that prohibited Methodists from participating in the slave trade, a decision that would later lead to division in the church. In addition, they added several doctrinal standards, including John Wesley's *Standard Sermons* and his *Notes Upon the New Testament.* The Christmas Conference marked the official organization of the American Methodist Church, which has since grown into numerous Methodist denominations. The conference also marked the beginning of the newly formed church's doctrinal standards and discipline which continue to be important guides for American Methodism today.

By this time, Wesley had accomplished many of his goals for the movement. He had consolidated the British and American Methodists and granted them the legal authority they needed to exist after his death. He had seen the movement spread throughout the British Isles and into North America in a relatively short time period. He had seen hundreds of thousands of souls come to Christ as a result of his ministry endeavors. He had created a class meeting system that would ensure his followers would continue to grow in the faith. And he had founded several educational institutions, leaving behind several written works which were intended to serve as a basis for the doctrine and discipline of his movement.

God with Us

Toward the end of his life, many of Wesley's close associates and friends, including his brother Charles, died. Despite these painful losses, Wesley was determined to continue the work of ministry until the very end of his life. He remarked that he did not want to be useless, and he continued to travel, preach, and oversee the Methodist movement. This quote gives a glimpse of the keen mind and wit Wesley still possessed at the age of eighty-five:

> I this day enter on my eighty-fifth year. And what cause have I to praise God, as for a thousand spiritual blessings, so for bodily blessings also! How little have I suffered yet, by the rush of numerous years! It is true, I am not so agile as I was in times past: I do not run or walk so fast as I did. My sight is a little decayed. My left eye is grown dim, and hardly serves me to read. . . . I find likewise some decay in my memory, with regard to names and things lately past; but not at all with regard to what I have read or heard twenty, forty, or sixty years ago.[1]

Wesley continued to preach and travel as planned until the very end of his life in February 1791. His final sermon was to a small group at Leatherhead, titled "Seek ye the Lord while He may be found, call ye upon Him while He is near." The following day, his mind as sharp as ever, he penned a letter to William Wilberforce, exhorting him to remain steadfast in his endeavors against slavery. Toward the end of the month, Wesley became very ill, and he returned to City Road to prepare for his death. Friends and family were called to say their last goodbyes. On the night of his death, he was heard to faintly whisper, "I'll praise, I'll praise." Then he said, "The best of all is God is with us." These were his last words. He then fell silent, passing away the next morning, March 2, 1791. He was eighty-eight years old. He was laid to rest in the cemetery at his chapel at City Road in London, and close to ten thousand people came to his funeral.

The true test of a leader is not how he starts the race, but how he finishes it, and it can be said that Wesley finished well. His final years were a period in which he worked tirelessly to strengthen and consolidate the advances of the Methodist revival. The organizational structures and the leadership team he pioneered would last long after his death. One mark of a great leader—and it takes great leaders for movements to happen—is his ability to ensure the organization will outlive him. One of the best testimonies to this fact is that it has now been over three hundred years since Wesley was born, and his legacy is still felt around the world. As we consider Wesley's life, we should ask ourselves as leaders, *What will I leave to the world when I die?* Wesley's challenge to us today is clear: "It matters not how long we live, but how well."

For a movement to survive and multiply, it must outlast its founding leaders. Jesus modeled this for us by training up apostles who would in turn lead the movement after his death and resurrection. Knowing he would not be physically present as the movement spread, he prepared men and women who would carry his message and vision from Jerusalem to the ends of the earth. In the book of Acts, we see the explosion of this multiplication movement under the leadership of the apostles. In a similar way, Wesley's legacy was not visible during his lifetime. Much of the growth of the movement occurred after his death. Today, nearly eighty million Christians around the world are a part of the broader Wesleyan tradition. Countless millions of others have been influenced by Wesley's teachings and his emphasis on discipleship, small groups, lay ministry, and innovative preaching.

Wesley's Lasting Legacy

Methodism miraculously grew from just a handful of students at Oxford College in 1726 to thousands of followers at the time of Wesley's death in 1791. And after Wesley's death, the British Methodists took steps to become fully autonomous from the Church of England. By 1836, Methodist preachers received full ordination, making the separation from the Church of England complete. In 1848, membership in Great Britain had grown to 338,861 and in Ireland to 23,842. As the years passed, the development and growth of British Methodism progressed, and today, as a result of British Methodism's missionary outreaches, there are Methodist conferences throughout the world. In the Pacific, there are independent conferences in Australia, New Zealand, and Tonga. Methodism in the West Indies is associated with Thomas Coke, who desired to take Methodism to the East but died at sea on his way to Ceylon (modern-day Sri Lanka) in 1814. His ministry companions established the work in Ceylon, which spread into India. In 1811, Sierra Leone became the site of the first Methodist work in West Africa, and in South Africa Methodism has an independent conference, which was established in 1882. Missions also came to Burma (known today as Myanmar) and China in the late 1800s. Today British Methodism has around 1.2 million members throughout its various churches. And the British Methodist movement has given birth to numerous other international denominations, which today number over 40 million people.

THE AFRICAN AMERICAN METHODIST CHURCHES

Early Methodists embraced diversity, and this gave rise to the African Methodist Episcopal Church, which began in 1787 in Philadelphia under the leadership of a black minister by the name of Richard Allen, a former slave. Allen was converted at the age of seventeen under Methodist preaching, and in 1781, he began preaching on Methodist circuits in Delaware and surrounding states. In 1786, he returned to Philadelphia and joined St. George's Methodist Church, where he helped provide leadership to a prayer service which drew dozens of blacks into the church.

Sadly, racial tensions increased. During a prayer service, a group of blacks sat in a pew that had been reserved for whites, and as they knelt and prayed, they were pulled from their knees and ordered to sit in their own area. After they finished prayer, the black Christians walked out the church and vowed never to return. Allen and several others felt it was time to form an independent church for blacks. Yet while Allen wanted black Christians to have their own place of worship, he didn't want to leave Methodism, saying: "The Methodists were the first people who brought glad tidings to the colored people. I feel thankful that ever I heard a Methodist preach. We are beholden to the Methodists, under God, for the light of the Gospel we enjoy; for all other denominations preached so high-flown that we were not able to comprehend their doctrine."[2]

Allen eventually purchased an old blacksmith's shop and used it as a house of worship. The church was formally organized in 1816 under his leadership. Bishop Francis Asbury dedicated the building and later ordained Allen. Yet despite efforts to keep the church a part of the Methodist Church, delegates from several black Methodist churches drafted their own "Ecclesiastical Compact," uniting them together as their own denomination, the African American Methodist Episcopal Church (AME).

The AME Church quickly grew to 7,500 members in the 1820s and would eventually become one of the largest Methodist churches in the United States, with nearly 3.3 million members in 7,200 churches. But it is not the only black Methodist denomination. The African Methodist Episcopal Zion Church dates from 1796. It was organized by a group protesting racial discrimination in New York. The first church in the group, named Zion, was built in 1800. The AME Zion Church held its first annual conference in 1821, and James Varick was elected the first bishop. The church spread quickly throughout the northern states, growing rapidly during the 1860s. Today, membership is comprised of nearly 1.2 million people in 3,000 churches worldwide.

OUTGROWTH OF THE WESLEYAN-HOLINESS MOVEMENT

Other groups formed from the Methodist church. During the 1800's several churches emerged which shared the same Wesleyan roots, including the Church of God (Anderson, Indiana), Church of the Nazarene, Church of God (Holiness), The Salvation Army, the Wesleyan Church, and the Free Methodist Church. All of these broke away from or grew out of the Wesleyan-Holiness Movement of the nineteenth century. These "Holiness Churches" placed a strong emphasis on Wesley's doctrine of sanctification and were loosely united by membership in the Christian Holiness Association, founded by a group of ministers after the Civil War to promote Christian holiness.

As I mentioned in an earlier chapter, the Pentecostal movement, which began in the early twentieth century, is in part descended from the Wesleyan-Holiness movement. Much research has been done to show the connections between the Wesleyan-Holiness movement and Pentecostalism. Some have even referred to John Wesley as the grandfather of Pentecostalism.[3] Today, Pentecostalism is the largest and fastest-growing Christian movement in the world.

The Spread of Wesleyanism

As we conclude our review of Wesley's lasting legacy and this brief look at some of the movements that grew out of Methodism, it is helpful to consider several of the reasons why the Methodist revival spread as widely and prolifically as it did in such a short amount of time.

FIRST, WESLEY HAD A BOLD VISION FOR THE SPREAD OF THE GOSPEL.

John Wesley had a distinct and intentional vision to spread and multiply Christianity through the Methodist movement. At one Methodist Conference he was asked, "What may we reasonably believe to be God's design in raising up the Preachers called Methodist?" Wesley's answer was thus: "To reform the nation, particularly the church, and to spread scriptural holiness over the land."[4] This vision to "spread   holiness over the land" gave Wesley's Methodists a distinctive identity and mission. While other traditions might trace their roots to confessional or theological systems, the Methodist movement was consciously evangelistic and missional, focused on preaching the gospel message in order to transform people's lives.

Similar multiplication language can be found throughout Wesley's letters, sermons, and journals. When writing about the Wesleyan revival, he often used words like "spread," "increase," and "advancement" to describe the growth and goals of Methodism. One of the convictions that drove his vision for multiplication was Wesley's belief that the growth of Methodism was a sovereign work of the Holy Spirit. He once declared, "It is plain to me that the whole work of God termed Methodism is an extraordinary dispensation of His providence."[5] Several of Wesley's sermons articulate his vision for globally spreading the Methodist revival. In the sermons, "On Laying the Foundation of the New Chapel" (1777) and "The Late Work of God in North America" (1778), Wesley described the progression in which Methodism spread throughout North America and the British Isles. It is clear that he believed the Spirit of God was doing an extraordinary work through the Methodist revival in America and England, and he associated this with "latter-day glory," a reference to the expectation of Christ's second coming. His focus went beyond the borders of England and America toward a global vision of salvation.

This emphasis on a universal or global work of the Spirit becomes even more evident in his sermon, "The General Spread of the Gospel" (1783). Therein, Wesley not only acknowledged the work of God in Great Britain, Ireland, and America, but also stated he believed it would spread throughout the world, speculating:

> Probably it will spread from these to the Protestants in France, to those in Germany, and to those in Switzerland; then Sweden, Denmark, Russia, and all other Protestant nations in Europe. May we not suppose that the same leaven of pure and undefiled religion, of the experimental knowledge and love of God, of inward and outward holiness, will afterwards spread to the Roman Catholics in Great Britain, Ireland, Holland;

in Germany, France, Switzerland. And may it gradually be diffused from provinces of Turkey, in Abyssinia, yea, and in the remotest parts, not only of Europe, but of Asia, Africa, and America? And in every nation under heaven, we may reasonably believe, God will observe the same order which he has done from the beginning.[6]

Wesley's universal vision of multiplication included people in every country and in every part of the world. In a sermon titled "The Signs of the Times" (1787), Wesley continued to describe his understanding of the growing spread of Methodism, comparing and contrasting the differences between the former religion (of the institutional church) and the latter-day glory, which was marked by an "extraordinary work of God." He called for Christians to discern the signs of the times, noting that the wise men of the world, men of eminence, men of learning and renown, cannot.[7] What did Wesley mean by "the signs of the times"? Wesley believed that the work of God would be marked by the universal spread of the gospel, which would be accompanied by:

> Inward and outward holiness, or "righteousness, and peace, and joy in the Holy Ghost," which "hath spread in various parts of Europe, particularly England, Scotland, Ireland, in the Islands, in the North and South, from Georgia to New England, and Newfoundland, that sinners have been truly converted to God, thoroughly changed both in heart and in life; not by tens, or by hundreds alone, but by thousands, yea, by myriads!"[8]

The rapid success and spread of the gospel were convincing signs of the times for Wesley. Not only was the gospel preached, but it resulted in genuine converts who were not only Christian in name (as in former times) but were "changed both in heart and life." The result was inward and outward holiness. The fruit of the Spirit authenticated the genuine conversion experience of the newly converted and contributed to the further spread of the gospel. In other words, true Christianity was seen as *contagious*. Wesley attributed this contagious nature to the extraordinary work of the Holy Spirit in the lives of people: "How swift, as well as how deep and how extensive, a work has been wrought in the present age! And certainly, not by might, neither by power, but by the Spirit of the Lord."[9] For Wesley, there was a clear connection between the way the Spirit works in personal salvation and the further spread of Christianity. Wesley's vision for multiplication was certainly for personal, individual transformation, but it also included a broader, worldwide perspective in which he envisioned the further spread of the Methodist movement.

Wesley defended the growth of Methodism, saying, "When hath religion, I will say not since the Reformation, but since the time of Constantine the Great, made so large a progress in any nation, within so short a space?"[10] Indeed, it is difficult to think of other movements that have had such an extensive advance in such a short period of time. Echoing Wesley, David Hempton says, "The rise of Methodism was the most important Protestant religious development since the Reformation."[11] As we consider our own context today and seek to learn from what has occurred in the past, Wesley reminds us that if we want to see a similar movement in our day, it ought to begin with a grand, biblically inspired vision for the spread of Christianity to the nations.

SECOND, WESLEY HAD AN INTENTIONAL STRATEGY FOR MULTIPLICATION.

As we saw earlier, Wesley was a master organizer and had an intentional strategy for multiplication of the Methodist movement that reproduced everything: disciples, leaders, bands, class meetings, societies, circuits, and conferences. Commenting on Wesley's intentional strategy for multiplication, George Hunter III writes, "He was instrumental in spawning many hundreds of classes, bands, societies, and other groups with distinct agendas, and he labored to develop the indigenous lay leaders that this growing vast network of groups would need."[12] As a result of this intentional strategy for multiplication, the Methodist movement continued to spread rapidly throughout the British Isles and North America. In his *Short History of the People Called Methodist*, Wesley writes plainly of his strategy for multiplication:

> About a hundred and thirty of my fellow-labourers are continually employed in the same thing. We all aim at one point, (as we did from the hour when we first engaged in the work), not at profit, any more than at ease, or pleasure, or the praise of men; but to spread true religion through London, Dublin, Edinburgh, and, as we are able, through the three kingdoms."[13]

Wesley wasn't seeking growth for the sake of growth itself, but in order to have a lasting impact on people's lives and to leave behind transformed communities. The "best way of spreading the gospel," Wesley concluded, was "to go a little and a little farther from London, Bristol, St. Ives, New Castle, or any other Society, So a little leaven would spread with more effect and less noise, and help would always be at hand."[14] This slow and steady method was his focus—not to cultivate large churches, but to raise up disciples who made disciples, slowly and strategically spreading intentional Christian community through the structured bands, class meetings, and societies. All of these connected people's lives together in a holistic discipleship ecosystem.

And though Wesley was not aiming for fast growth, under his supervision, Methodism grew steadily and gradually, eventually becoming one of the fastest-growing movements the Western world has ever seen. This is the power of exponential multiplication. By 1768, after thirty years of multiplication, Methodism had 40 circuits and 217,341 members. Ten years later, that number had grown to 60 circuits and 40,089 members. In another decade, there were 99 circuits and 66,375 members. And by 1798, seven years after Wesley's death, the numbers had jumped to 149 circuits and 101,712 members. Howard Snyder comments, "This is the stuff church growth charts are made of! Yet the growth was gradual and measured, not explosive or dramatic, for Wesley was building disciples rather than seeking impressive numbers."[15]

PROFILE

Global Church Planting Movements

Church planting movements are happening all around the world, changing entire countries with the gospel of Jesus Christ. David Garrison is a leading expert in this area, and he defines a church planting movement as "a rapid and multiplicative increase of indigenous churches planting churches within a given people group or population segment." Garrison served as the associate vice president for global strategy with the Southern Baptist International Mission Board (IMB) for five years and studied mission outreach in more than 180 countries. With the help of the IMB's global research department, Garrison was able to make in–depth studies of some of the world's fastest-growing Christian movements. In his book, *Church Planting Movements: How God Is Redeeming A Lost World,* he examines more than two dozen movements of multiplying churches on five continents.

Consider the following examples from his research.

A church planting movement among the Bhojpuri people of India resulted in more than 4,000 new churches and some 300,000 new believers.

A church planting movement in Outer Mongolia produced more than 10,000 converts while a subsequent movement in Inner Mongolia resulted in some 50,000 new believers.

A church planting movement in one Latin American country increased the total number of churches from 129 to more than 2,600 in a decade, an increase of more than 1,900 percent.

A church planting movement in a northern Chinese province produced 20,000 new believers and 500 new churches planted in less than five years.

Chinese Christians in Qing'an County of Heilongjiang Province planted 236 new churches in a single month.

In southern China, a church planting movement produced more than 90,000 baptized believers in 920 house churches in eight years.

In 2002, one church planting movement produced 15,000 new churches and 160,000 baptized believers in a single year.

After presenting these case studies, Garrison identifies ten universal elements present in each movement:

1. *Prayer.* Prayer in our personal lives and corporate life that has such vitality, it leads to imitation.
2. *Abundant gospel sowing.* In church planting movements, hundreds and even thousands of individuals are hearing the claim Jesus Christ has on their lives.
3. *Intentional church planting.* In every church planting movement, someone implemented a strategy of deliberate church planting before the movement got underway.
4. *Scriptural authority.* The Bible was almost always translated into the language of the people.
5. *Local leadership.* Missionaries must have the self-discipline required to mentor church planters rather than do the job of church planting themselves.
6. *Lay leadership.* Church planting movements are driven by lay and bi-vocational leaders. This reliance upon lay leadership ensures the largest pool of potential church planters and house church leaders.
7. *Cell or house churches.* Church buildings do appear in church planting movements. However, the vast majority of the churches continue to be small, reproducible cell churches of 10–30 members meeting in homes and storefronts.
8. *Churches planting churches.* In most church planting movements, the first churches were planted by missionaries. At some point, however, as the movements entered a multiplicative phase of repro-

duction, the churches themselves began planting churches.

9. *Rapid reproduction.* When rapid reproduction is taking place, you can be assured that the churches are unencumbered by nonessentials and the laity are fully empowered to participate in this work of God.

10. *Healthy churches.* Many of the churches involved in church planting movements demonstrate vital marks of a healthy church.[16]

The Spread of American Methodism

The amazing spread of Methodism in the United States wasn't fully realized until after Wesley's death. Under the leadership of Francis Asbury, American Methodism grew from a few thousand adherents to the largest denomination in the land, even surpassing in size its nearest rival, the Baptists, by twenty percent. American Methodism had as many members as the Episcopalians, Congregationalists, and Presbyterians combined. When Asbury arrived in the US in 1784, there were a few hundred Methodists in America. By the time of his death in 1816, there were over two hundred thousand American Methodists.[17] Fifty years after Methodism came to America, more than a quarter of all professing Christians in America belonged to the Methodist Episcopal Church, and the percentage of Methodists continued to grow at the same ratio until the end of the nineteenth century. By 1908, Methodism had almost nine million members and at least four times as many adherents. There were 150 thousand ministers and lay preachers, and thousands of schools, seminaries, and colleges around the world. From 1880 to 1905, American Methodism averaged planting over seven hundred churches per year. That's an amazing story of church growth!

The growth of Methodism in North America eclipsed the growth of Methodism in England and other parts of the world. As Roger Finke and Rodney Starke noted, "Methodism in Great Britain floundered while American Methodism soared. As the Methodists in Great Britain struggled to keep pace with population growth, the percentage of Methodists in America continued to climb."[18] There are various reasons for this, but one key reason was the pioneering spirit of American Methodism that allowed it to flourish as a grassroots movement on the open frontier. Missionary zeal and a passion for souls remained at the heart of the movement. The early American Methodists traveled through dangerous new frontiers and uncharted territories to reach people with the gospel of Jesus Christ. Their circuit riders braved the rigors of the wild frontier, facing hunger, bad weather, attacks, and illness. Many of them did not live past the age of thirty. Consider the account of pioneer Methodist Freeborn Garrettson, whose words demonstrate the sacrifice, commitment, and dedication the early Methodist circuit riders had in reaching souls for Christ:

> I traversed the mountains and valleys, frequently on foot, with my knapsack on my back, guided by Indian paths in the wilderness, when it was not expedient to take a horse. I had often to ride through morasses, half deep in mud and water frequently satisfying my hunger with a piece of bread and pork from my knapsack, quenching my thirst from a brook, and resting my weary limbs on the leaves of trees. Thanks be to God! He compensated me for my toil; for many precious souls were awakened and converted to God.[19]

Like Wesley before him, Francis Asbury embodied this missionary legacy to the American Methodists and became known as "America's Bishop." After forty years of ministry, he wrote in 1815, "The Methodist preachers, who had been sent by John Wesley to America, came as Missionaries and now, behold the consequences of this mission. We have seven hundred travelling preachers, and three thousand local preachers, who cost us nothing. We will not give up the cause—we will not abandon the world to infidels."[20]

Conclusion

Thanks to Wesley's original vision for spreading the gospel around the world and the work and dedication of Francis Asbury, Methodism became one of the most dynamic movements in all of church history. The influence of Methodism went well beyond the Methodist church and influenced many other religious movements within North America and around the world. Commenting on the lasting influence of the movement, John Wigger wrote, "Methodism's theology, worship style, and system of discipline worked their ways deep into the fabric of American life, influencing nearly all other mass religious movements that would follow, as well as many facets of American life not directly connected to the church."[21] Perhaps more than any other Christian denomination in the West, Methodism will be remembered as a multiplication movement, one that spread the gospel from England to the world.

The Wesleyan revival grew out of a bold vision to spread and multiply the gospel through disciples, leaders, bands, class meetings, and churches, and then grew into a global phenomenon. What the church needs now is a similar vision for multiplication to combat its rapid decline in the West. I believe the West can see a movement once again if we will embrace the vision, spirit, and sacrifice that drove John Wesley, Francis Asbury, and the early Methodists. Organic multiplication is a part of our Christian heritage, and can be a part of the church today, if we are willing to reclaim it.

As we have seen, revival movements are not the creation of human beings, but the work of God as he is moving in and through his church all around the world. The good news is that God has not forgotten the Western church, and there are signs of hope springing up all around the United States and Great Britain. It's happening all around us: in people's homes, in coffee shops, and maybe on your street corner.

CHAPTER 8

MOVEMENTS CAN BE MESSY

*While we need the past, we must not let
ourselves become imprisoned by it or allow it to
become an idol.*

ESTHER DE WAAL

After reading about the rapid growth of the Methodist movement, one might be tempted to think it was a perfect movement. However, as I stated in the introduction, movements are messy, and early Methodism was no exception. We tend to learn more from our mistakes than we do from our successes, so there are benefits in considering some of the flaws of the Wesleyan revival. We can learn vital lessons from the movement's weaknesses as well as from its strengths.

Wesley's Personal Life

Although John Wesley was well-respected as a leader whose life was marked by personal piety and prayer, his marriage was, by all accounts, a disaster. In 1748, Wesley intended to marry Grace Murray, a Methodist widow who had previously been a housekeeper and was considerably younger than him. Charles Wesley did not approve of the relationship because he felt Grace was not the right woman for Wesley. Charles convinced her to marry another Methodist preacher by the name of John Bennet. Needless to say, Wesley was very upset over the matter. The event was a scandal and led to a division between the two brothers.

In response, Wesley hastily married Mary Vazeille in February 1751. She was a wealthy widow, but after several years of marriage, they began to have serious problems. Wesley spent most of his time and attention on promoting the spread of Methodism, and Mary became jealous of his tireless work and close friendships with certain Methodist women. Her jealousy may not have been altogether unjustified. Wesley worked day and night and had little time for a stay-at-home wife. Wesley and Mary were separated on several occasions, and perhaps most shocking of all, when she died, he was out of town. He did not even attend her funeral.

This is one of the areas of Wesley's life that should be examined and even criticized. Granted, we should acknowledge that the sheer demand of Wesley's apostolic work would have put a strain on any marriage. Yet it's also interesting to note that someone who seemed to be so successful, so pious, and so well-respected had a dark corner in his life. This isn't to cast doubt on Wesley's sincerity or his spirituality, but it is a reminder that people are fallible and movements are complex, yet despite those complexities, God is faithful, and he uses imperfect people.

Division and Lack of Unity

Methodism was not always a unified movement, and during its early years, two camps emerged from the revival at Oxford, one Calvinist and the other Arminian. George Whitefield was the leader of the Calvinist wing, and he and his followers embraced a set of doctrines developed by followers of the reformer John Calvin. These teachings emphasized that all humanity is depraved, there is unconditional election for the saved, atonement is limited to the chosen, God's grace is irresistible, and saints will persevere to the end. These views were in conflict with Wesley's doctrine of free grace, which taught that salvation was available to all men and women, not just the elect.[1] Wesley made it clear that his teaching was not an endorsement of any inherent good in humanity; rather, it was an affirmation that God's saving grace is extended to all persons, allowing them to choose whether to believe the gospel or not.

These doctrinal differences led to a split between Wesley and Whitefield, but they highlight an important lesson we can learn from Wesley: his unique ability to find a middle way between radical extremes and paradoxes. Wesley, in articulating his differences from Whitefield and the Calvinists, sought to hold extremes such as divine sovereignty and free will, evangelicalism and sacramentalism, and saving and sanctifying grace all in tension with one another. Wesley believed we must live in the tension of the paradoxes of the Christian faith without letting the mystery of God's work undermine our faith. He maintained a gracious stance and said of those who were not opposed to the orthodox essentials of Christianity, "We should think and let think."[2] He also said, "Is thy heart right, as my heart is with thine? I ask no farther question. If it be, give me thy hand. For opinions, or terms, let us not destroy the work of God. Dost thou love and serve God? It is enough. I give thee the right hand of fellowship."[3] His willingness to seek fellowship, even with those who differed doctrinally from his own views, is an example we can learn from today. In the end, John Wesley and George Whitefield reconciled their friendship. In fact, Wesley even preached the sermon at Whitefield's funeral, a beautiful picture of reconciliation between the two men.

I'm hopeful that Wesley's manner of dealing with doctrinal differences might provide a model for reconciliation between doctrinally diverse Christian traditions today. Wesley emphasized what we can agree on—the essentials of the faith—and sought to join together with others in a common mission to reach our world for Christ. I believe it is possible for those in Wesleyan and Reformed backgrounds to learn from one another and work together for the sake of the kingdom of God, despite their theological differences. As Roger Olson reminds us, the evangelical community needs both George Whitefield and John Wesley in order to achieve the beauty of balance.[4] To that I offer a hearty, "Amen!"

Institutionalization and Secularization

While there is much we can learn from how Wesley handled theological disagreements with others, perhaps the greatest warning we can take from the success of the Wesleyan revival is to observe what can happen to a movement over time. Sadly, some movements, as they become institutionalized, also grow more secular, losing the "evangelical" focus that gave them life in the first place. Many denominations that began as an evangelical or evangelistic movement eventually became institutionalized, leaving behind their evangelical roots. If the cultural values and beliefs that initially helped the movement grow are not passed down to succeeding generations, this institutionalization will lead to the loss of the gospel focus and of disciple-making. C. S. Lewis warned against this, saying, "There exists in every church something that sooner or later works against the very purpose for which it came into existence. So we must strive very hard, by the grace of God to keep the church focused on the mission that Christ originally gave it."[5] The cure for this secularization of the revival spirit, as Lewis suggests, is to develop habits and practices that keep us faithful to the original mission of the church: the call to preach the gospel and make disciples.

We see this pattern repeated throughout history. Many of the great revivals of the past began as Spirit-inspired disciple-making movements, yet over time they became secular institutions. For example, consider the history of the modern university.[6] Many colleges, including state universities in the United States, started out as Christian institutions to train young people for ministry and Christian service. Schools like Harvard (Puritan), William and Mary (Anglican), Yale (Congregational), and Princeton (Presbyterian) were created for Christian higher education.[7] The Great Awakening led to the founding of Princeton, Brown, Rutgers, and Dartmouth in the mid-eighteenth century, and to the single most prolific period of college founding in American history.[8] Over time, however, the revival spirit that founded these institutions was lost, and most of these former Christian colleges and universities became secular universities with little or no religious affiliation.[9]

Methodism was one of the greatest and longest-lasting discipleship movements in the history of the church. Yet as Methodism continued to grow, Wesley noticed that the movement was following the patterns of institutionalization. He lamented that this was happening, and he felt that a grim fate might befall the Methodists if they ever lost their zeal. Wesley wrote:

I am not afraid that the people called Methodists should ever cease to exist either in Europe or America. But I am afraid, lest they should only exist as a dead sect, having the form of religion without the power. And this undoubtedly will be the case, unless they hold fast the doctrine, spirit, and discipline with which they first set out.[10]

Sadly, this is exactly what happened to Methodism in the United States. Just one hundred years after the miraculous growth of the movement, there were warning signs of secularization. Today, the United Methodist Church, the descendant of the American Methodist movement, is in rapid decline and on the verge of splitting into factions. What caused this shift, making a large and growing denomination one of the fastest declining?

History teaches us that the church is susceptible to the secularizing tendencies of institutionalization whenever it loses focus on the message and mission of Christ. As Alvin Reid and Mark Liederbach have said, "When the church loses, forgets, or fails to emphasize the missional thrust of its purpose . . . it is a move away from a movement mentality toward what we would describe as institutionalism."[11] Whenever movements are transformed into institutional churches, they will begin to reduce the tension they feel with respect to the surrounding culture. There is less emphasis placed on growth and multiplication, and this leads to a loss of growth and the start of a slow decline.[12] This pattern has repeated over and over again throughout the history of the church. And while there are many sociological factors to consider, there are three primary reasons this secularization occurred in the Methodist movement, leading to its decline in North America.

FACTOR 1: THE EDUCATION OF CLERGY

The first factor contributing to secularization was the clergy becoming more educated. To be clear, there is nothing wrong with pursuing education, and in most cases it is good to have an educated clergy. Yet as Methodism became an established church in North America, there was a strong impulse to "keep up" with the more established churches and to become a respectable part of society. This led to a strong push to send preachers to seminary. Though the movement had grown and multiplied through lay preachers and circuit riders, the days of the traveling preacher on horseback were now replaced by fancy pulpits and robes. More and more Methodist churches desired educated clergy. Clergy supported this, as more education brought with it higher social status and increased pay. When Francis Asbury died in 1816, there was not a single Methodist college or seminary in the United States. Yet by 1880 there were 11 theological seminaries, 44 colleges and universities, and 130 women's seminaries and schools.[13] According to Methodist historian William Warren Sweet, "Clergy culture and learning were no longer a monopoly of the Congregationalists, the Presbyterians, and the Episcopalians. Education, refinement, and dignity now characterized the ministry and service of the Methodists."[14]

With this increased emphasis on higher education came a shift in the preaching. Educated clergy moved away from simple messages on sin and salvation to speak about science and politics. Gone were the days of the Methodist camp meeting. Early Methodist preachers had arisen from among the common people, speaking the language of the ordinary man. A generation later, pulpits were filled with educated clergy who geared their message to a more educated, socially conscious audience.

FACTOR 2: CLASS CHANGE

The shift in clergy education led to churches becoming more upper and middle class in membership. One hundred years from its humble beginnings, Methodism in North America had finally arrived. Not only had the Methodists become the largest denomination in the land, they had moved up the social ladder of society and were beginning to attract people of wealth and privilege. They had shifted from meeting in simple, unadorned buildings to building large, expensive facilities that rivaled the nicest established church buildings in town. A new building for First Methodist Church in Evanston, Illinois even began charging $200 for good seats at the church!

These new, fancy buildings were a visible sign that Methodism had moved away from the vision of its founder. Once an upstart sect, it had become one of the established religions of the young nation. Yet while some would see these as positive signs, they were the beginning of the end of the Methodist movement in North America. Today, you can look at almost any town in North America and find an impressive Methodist church building from this era, yet sadly, most of these have closed or are in the process of closing their doors due to declining membership.

FACTOR 3: A CHANGE IN SPIRIT

Over time the pioneering, counter-cultural spirit of the Methodist movement was domesticated. With the rise of educated clergy and increased social status came a further shift away from the original emphasis on holiness and the "methods" of the class meeting. As Finke and Stark note, "Their clergy were increasingly willing to condone the pleasures of this world and to de-emphasize sin, hell-fire, and damnation; this lenience struck highly responsive cords in an increasingly affluent, influential, and privileged membership. This is, of course, the fundamental dynamic by which sects are transformed into churches, thereby losing the vigor and the high-octane faith that caused them to succeed in the first place."[15] The nail in the coffin was the demise of the class meeting. From the time of the founding of Methodism, to be called a Methodist meant that you were a member of a class meeting. Yet over time this requirement was lost, and many began to see it as a sign that the movement had begun to falter. In 1856, at the age of seventy-two and in the fifty-third year of his ministry, the famous Methodist circuit rider preacher Peter Cartwright was already lamenting the loss of the class meeting:

> Class meetings have been owned and blessed of God in the Methodist Episcopal Church . . . For many years we kept them with closed doors, and suffered none to remain in class meeting more than twice or thrice unless they signified a desire to join the Church . . . Here the hard heart has been tendered, the cold heart warmed with the holy fire; But how sadly are the class meetings neglected in the Methodist Episcopal Church! . . . Is it any wonder that so many of our members grow cold and careless in religion, and finally back-slide? . . . And now, before God, are not many of our preachers at fault in this matter?[16]

Reading Cartwright's words, one can sense the grief of a man who had experienced the exciting energy of the Methodist revival and was now seeing that movement sliding toward institutionalization and into decline. As I mentioned earlier, on my desk is a framed class meeting ticket from 1842 that belonged to a woman named Maria Snyder. Looking at it today, I can't help but wonder, "What would Maria think of contemporary Methodism?" or "What would John Wesley or Francis Asbury think about the current state of the movement they started?"

While more can be said, I believe the lesson we can learn from this is clear. We need to take a hard look in the mirror and ask ourselves if we are in danger of repeating the same mistakes. Across the Western world, thousands of churches are closing every year. When will we feel grief over the state of our churches? Will a new generation once again heed the call to recover Scriptural Christianity? Might we see another disciple-making revolution spread across our country and around the world?

Conclusion

Let me end this chapter with a question that may already be on your mind: Is spiritual renewal possible for existing churches or mainline denominations that are stagnant or in decline? I believe the answer is yes. One of the most exciting examples of renewal is happening today, somewhat ironically, within the Church of England, the very church that turned John Wesley out over three hundred years ago. In the midst of rapid decline in church attendance nationally, there is a multiplication movement brewing in the Church of England that is bringing renewal to churches and communities across England.

In 2015, the former Bishop of London Richard Chartres delivered a lecture entitled "New Fire in London" in which he talked about the growth within the Diocese of London through church planting. He shared the following commitment to mission: "We are pledged to establish 100 new worshipping communities in the Diocese in the next five years."[17] To help accomplish this vision, Ric Thorpe was consecrated as Bishop of Islington with a special focus on church planting in London. Thorpe oversees London's church growth strategy to plant one hundred churches in London by 2020 and two hundred city-center church-planting churches around the country by 2030.

Thorpe's passion is to make disciple-making leaders in new and revitalized churches in London and across England. "My main work is culture change," he says. "I'm trying to help people imagine themselves more as a missionary church, as opposed to just sustaining what has always gone before." Thorpe helps churches discover and pray into God's vision for their future, whether that's growing themselves, planting a new church, or revitalizing declining churches. "I'm energized by spending time with people who feel God's call to go somewhere else and do something new," he says. "Just to spend time with them and to help them articulate the plans that God has for them and to work out what they need to do to go to the next level, and to help them think through what might be next on the horizon."[18] His goal is not just to have a growing church, but to see disciples, leaders, and churches that multiply everywhere. Thorpe reminds me of John Wesley in many ways!

Once again, let us revisit Howard Snyder's five dimensions of renewal movements from chapter 1: personal, corporate, conceptual, structural, and missiological. This paradigm offers us a helpful way to understanding how renewal comes to the church. We can see these five dimensions at work throughout various historic renewal movements and in the lives of reformers and visionaries like Luther, Calvin, Wycliffe, Wesley—and even modern-day examples like Ric Thorpe.

First, if we want to see church renewal happen today, it needs to begin with us—with an experience of personal and spiritual renewal that comes through prayer and the work of the Holy Spirit. We have to first experience the change we want to see in the church and the world, which means it starts with you and me. You can't share what you haven't experienced yourself!

Second, if we want to see renewal, it must become corporate and spread to the whole body of Christ. We need to cultivate vital, generative relationships with other Christians who share a similar vision for change and church renewal. We can't do it alone; we need men and women who will link arms with us in the long, hard work of church renewal. Movements are not simply ideas; they are a work by and for the people, and it takes vital relationships to make movements happen.

Third, renewal often comes conceptually, through a fresh vision of what the church could and should be. If we wish to prepare our hearts for a fresh movement of God's Spirit, we need a fresh vision for what renewal, discipleship, and church multiplication could look like in our context. As we just saw, one of the most important things Ric Thorpe does is help churches discover and pray into God's vision for their future.

Fourth, there needs to be structural renewal to support and strengthen the ongoing work of renewal. The Wesleyan revival is an excellent example of structural renewal. Wesley's discipleship systems provided the structural support the revival needed. Many revival movements die out quickly because they never develop the structures they need to continue to grow and multiply in a healthy way.

Fifth, renewal needs to become missiological to be biblically dynamic. We see this clearly with what is happening in the Church of England today. Ric is helping lead a renewal movement from within the church that exists for mission and church planting. What began in the hearts of a few individuals has spread to planting dozens of new faith communities across England.

Finally, if we want to see renewal, we must seek the God of renewal. Movements are not the result of our labor, but of the sovereign work of the Holy Spirit. We must learn from the examples of the past, from leaders like John Wesley, who successfully stewarded the fires of revival into a worldwide multiplication movement. God did it once. He can do it again today.

THE NEW MISSION FRONTIER

I have but one passion: It is He, it is He alone.
The world is the field and the field is the world;
and henceforth that country shall be my home
where I can be most used in winning souls for
Christ.

COUNT ZINZENDORF

This book is an invitation to look back—to the Wesleyan revival, drawing wisdom and inspiration from the past—and to look forward as we seek to make disciples today. I recently taught the ideas in this book to a group of pastors and leaders. During that time, Kim Gladding, Director for Discipleship for the Wesleyan Church, made a comment that has stuck with me.

She said, "Recovering the foundation of the Wesleyan movement is going back to the future." And I'm convinced she is correct.

I hope you have been blessed to learn more about John Wesley and the Methodist movement. But my reason for writing this is not to encourage us to slavishly copy the methods, terminology, and traditions of Wesley and his followers. Many denominations and churches find themselves stuck in the past, thinking that if they can return to the "good ol' days," everything will be right again. Perpetuating the successes of the past is not a recipe for future success in a changing world. But there is something we can learn. We can embrace the spirit behind the movement and take the principles of past movements—what I am calling the "marks of a movement"—and let those timeless truths shape our methods, practices, and movements today.

This book is not seeking to advocate a specific church tradition, nor am I attempting to create a new denomination. Truthfully, I don't think we should even have one specific style or model of church ministry. I'm simply trying to draw our attention to a handful of time-honored movemental practices that made the Wesleyan revival successful. What you do with these lessons and how you apply them in your context is up to you.

It may be helpful to remember that for Wesley, Methodism was not a new denomination—it was simply a call to radical discipleship. Wesley desired the renewal of all denominations, especially his own, the Church of England. He once wrote a tract entitled, "The Character of a Methodist," wherein he offered several marks of true Christians that would distinguish them from the world: "By these marks, by these fruits of a living faith, do we labor to distinguish ourselves from the unbelieving world . . . But from real Christians, of whatsoever denomination they be, we earnestly desire not to be distinguished at all."[1] While Wesley's hope was that these things would mark the Methodist movement, his vision was the recovery of genuine Christianity more broadly. Wesley's vision was not denominational, it was a universal vision of what it means to follow Jesus in every place, in every culture, in every generation.

I was recently interviewed by Daniel Yang, the director of the Send Network, a church planting and missionary organization. Reflecting on my research into the growth of the Methodist movement in the frontiers of the American colonies, Daniel asked if I saw similar "frontiers" today, places and people for the church to reach in a new way with a fresh message. My response? I believe the new frontier of Christianity in the United States is less of a rugged frontier. It's distinctly urban and multiethnic.

I say this because we cannot ignore the reality that immigration is reshaping the United States. Currently, about forty-three million residents were born in another country and have immigrated to the United States. With over 337 languages, the United States has become the most multicultural and multilingual nation on earth. In addition, it is estimated that 50 percent of the world will live in or near urban centers by 2050 and 75 percent will work and live in cities. Cities provide easy access to reach people living in large geographic regions in and near major cities. Cities are also mosaics made up of many different ethnic people groups that are open to the gospel. The result of these converging trends is a need for new urban churches, churches that are intentionally multiethnic and multicultural.

Could this be the new frontier for a revival movement? I'm hopeful. These churches provide a beautiful picture of the kingdom of God. As the apostle Paul reminds us, the gospel calls us to sacrifice our own interests, desires, and privileges for the sake of others and for unity in the love of Christ. Paul writes, "I have become all things to all people, that by all means I might save some. I do it all for the sake of the gospel, that I may share with them in its blessings" (1 Cor. 9:22b–23 ESV). Multicultural, multiethnic churches point us to the beautiful picture promised in Revelation, where people from every nation, tribe, people, and language praise God in unison with one another. Regardless of the type of church we currently attend or are thinking about planting, I think we should all be looking for ways to reach across ethnic, racial, cultural, and economic barriers. As our culture is changing, I believe multiculturalism and multiethnicity will be the future of church planting in North America and the world.

Even now, we see a growing number of new churches adopting this focus on reaching people from various nationalities and ethnic backgrounds. In many urban contexts, church plants must, of necessity, cross racial, cultural, and socioeconomic lines to reach their communities. One example of this is my friend Anderson Moyo, who pastors a multiethnic church called Sheffield Community Church in England. Originally from Zimbabwe, Anderson has a heart not only for Europe, but also for the Africans who have come to England. He says, "We hope to train not only Africans, but emerging leaders from across the world as our denomination expands to new frontiers beyond the Western hemisphere."

Another example of an urban church movement happening here in my own backyard is Fuente De Avivamiento (Spring of Revival), which is led by my friend Dr. Iosmar Alvarez in Lexington, Kentucky. Fuente De Avivamiento bears all the marks of the Wesleyan movement that we have examined throughout this book, and like Wesley, the movement began when Iosmar had a **life-changing encounter** with the Lord. Iosmar was born and raised in Cuba and became a veterinarian. Yet all his worldly ambitions changed when he was gloriously saved during a Methodist crusade in Cuba. When Iosmar came to the United States, he sensed the Lord calling him to plant churches—not just one church, but a whole movement of new churches with a Wesleyan DNA. Since planting Fuente in Lexington, that single church has become a **contagious movement** reaching hundreds of people in the Latino community. Every week new people come to faith in Christ, and the church is teeming with the presence and power of the Holy Spirit.

Members of the church have a fervent spirituality that is **Spirit-filled** and marked by a hunger for the Word of God and prayer. They have developed an **organic discipleship ecosystem** that keeps their members connected and committed in active discipleship. They gather across the city once a week in nearly one hundred groups that meet in people's homes for worship, teaching, and prayer ministry. Fuente's house churches function just like the class meetings of early Methodism, which met in people's homes throughout the week. They are committed to holistic mission by caring for people's felt needs.

Their growing movement has an apostolic DNA that is especially committed to **empowering non-ordained people** to do the work of the ministry. Their leaders are ordinary women and men who work ordinary jobs throughout the week but also serve as the pastors of their house churches. As they demonstrate faithfulness in their house churches, some eventually become leaders over ministries and others are sent out to plant churches across the region. Finally, they are reproducing themselves through **organic multiplication**, planting several other churches across the Lexington area and helping launch a national network of churches being planted all across the country.

Throughout this book, I have presented the key marks of a movement based on the Wesleyan revival, which I believe can lead to multiplication movements today. In many ways, these marks have been alive in the apostolic DNA of the church in every generation of believers since the time of Christ, and they are alive in the church today. They are common essentials for making disciples—whether you lived in the first century or live in the twenty-first century—and we as the church must recover their power.

But we must not forget that every movement and every context is unique. The Methodist movement successfully responded to the unique needs of its time with the timeless gospel of Jesus Christ. In a similar way, we must seek to understand our unique context and culture, to bring God's timeless Word to a changing culture. As theologian Francis Schaeffer reminds us, "Every generation of Christians has this problem of learning how to speak meaningfully to its own age. It cannot be solved without an understanding of the changing existential situation which it faces."[2]

Today, there are many different expressions of the local church, which represent the body of Christ in a variety of contexts. The church in Africa looks different than the church in Texas; each one is called to be the church in its unique context and culture. Over the last few years I have been able to experience many new contextualized churches around the world in cities, in jungles, and on the tops of mountains. I have met with church leaders from five continents. Each church I experienced was a little different from the others, but they all had one thing in common: they were all members of the body of Jesus Christ. These experiences have profoundly shaped my vision of the need for a new contextualized movement that is unique for the day and time in which we live.

My prayer is that in some small way, reading this book has led you to draw inspiration from the Wesleyan movement. I hope and pray that in learning about John Wesley, the Spirit will spark a similar multiplication movement yet again. May the Sovereign Lord do something powerful again in our day!

I close with a version of John Wesley's covenant prayer. It's a prayer I pray almost daily, and over the last few years it has inspired my faith and witness to seek God for a fresh revival movement in my lifetime.

I am no longer my own, but thine.
Put me to what thou wilt, rank me with whom thou wilt.
Put me to doing, put me to suffering.
Let me be employed for thee or laid aside for thee,
exalted for thee or brought low for thee.
Let me be full, let me be empty.
Let me have all things, let me have nothing.
I freely and heartily yield all things to thy pleasure and disposal.
And now, O glorious and blessed God, Father, Son and Holy
  Spirit,
thou art mine, and I am thine.
So be it.
And the covenant which I have made on earth,
let it be ratified in heaven.
Amen.

AFTERWORD

My friend Winfield Bevins has rightly reminded us of the vital multiplication lessons from the Wesleyan movement, one of the greatest missional movements the world has ever known. Every missional movement appears to observers as simple disciple-making systems. Yet importantly, these movements intentionally retain disciple-making as a core practice. Discipleship is at once the starting point, the abiding strategic practice—and the key to all lasting missional impact in and through movements. Whether one looks at the Wesleyan, Franciscan, or Chinese phenomena, all of them are at the core essentially composed of (and led by) disciples, and they are absolutely clear about this disciple-making mandate.

The Methodist movement, as this book has described in detail, is an excellent example of this. It began in eighteenth-century Britain when, following a life-changing encounter with God, John Wesley began to travel throughout Great Britain with a vision for the conversion and discipling of the nation and the renewal of a fallen church. He "sought no less than the recovery of the truth, life, and power of earliest Christianity and the expansion of that kind of Christianity." Within a generation, one in thirty people living in Britain had become Methodists, and the movement quickly became a worldwide phenomenon. In the opinion of Stephen Addison, a missiologist who has spent much of his professional life studying Christian movements, the key to Methodism's success was the high level of commitment to the Methodist cause expected of participants.

The Methodist cause declined to the degree that the movement shifted away from its original missional ethos of evangelism and disciple-making and degenerated into mere religious legalism maintained by institution, rule books, and highly professionalized clergy. In fact, although Methodism in America had experienced massive exponential growth—35 percent of the population in around forty years—two critical "movement killers" were introduced into Methodism in America that effectively hamstrung the movement. The first started in 1850, when the leaders of Methodism had tired of the Episcopalians and the Presbyterians who were deriding them as "uncouth and unlearned" ministers. They decided that all their circuit riders and local ministers had to complete four years of ordination studies in order to qualify. Growth ceased straightaway! Then, ten years later (in 1860), they no longer required classes and bands—discipleship had become an optional extra. Methodism has been in decline ever since!

As Bevins reminds us in the conclusion, we should not simply pay attention to the marks that led the movement to multiply, we should also pay attention to the movement killers. One "killer" was the requirement of ordination studies for clergy to do what every believer already receives at his or her conversion—the agency and ministry of all believers. The second "killer," of course, is a lack of discipleship. Most churches in the West have followed this path. Any guesses about what has to change?

Marks of a Movement doesn't provide us with all the answers, but it calls us back to the disciple-making mandate of the church by reminding us of the timeless wisdom of John Wesley and the Methodist movement. With a love for history and a passion for today's church, Winfield Bevins has helped us reimagine church multiplication in a way that focuses on making and multiplying disciples for the twenty-first century.

Alan Hirsch, author of *The Forgotten Ways*

APPENDIX A

THE DISCIPLESHIP BAND MEETING

A discipleship band is a group of 3–5 people who read together, pray together and meet together to become the love of God for one another and the world.

Taken from *Discipleship Bands: A Practical Field Guide*. Visit DiscipleshipBands.com for more.

The Opening (after some banter and small talk)

ONE VOICE: Awake O Sleeper and Rise from the Dead.
ALL OTHERS: And Christ Will Shine on You.

(Adapted from Ephesians 4:14)

PRAYER (READ IN UNISON OR BY ONE MEMBER OF THE BAND)

Heavenly Father, we pray that out of your glorious riches you would strengthen us with power through your Spirit in our inner being, so that Christ may dwell in our hearts through faith. And we pray that we, being rooted and established in love, may have power, together with all the Lord's holy people, to grasp how wide and long and high and deep is the love of Christ, and to know this love that surpasses knowledge—that we may be filled to the measure of all the fullness of God. We ask this in Jesus' name, amen.

(ADAPTED FROM EPHESIANS 3:16–19)

The Five Questions

1. HOW IS IT WITH YOUR SOUL?

This is the locater question. Where are you? How are you doing on the inside? Downcast? Joy-filled? Weary? Well?

2. WHAT ARE YOUR STRUGGLES AND SUCCESSES?

Peel back a layer of life and talk about circumstances, difficulties, challenges, successes, satisfying growth and such.

3. ANY SIN TO CONFESS?

This takes courage. Just put it out there. No questions asked. Allow someone from the band to say to you: "In the name of Jesus Christ, you are forgiven." Then receive it.

4. ANYTHING YOU WANT TO KEEP SECRET?

The answer can be no, yes, or yes and . . . Again, no condemnation. This question will take the band to the next level.

5. HOW MIGHT THE HOLY SPIRIT BE SPEAKING AND MOVING IN YOUR LIFE?

Risk sharing a possibility of what God might be doing. Invite the band to share their discernment from what they are hearing, too. After each person shares, someone else in the band offers prayer for them. When all have shared and been prayed for, the meeting is ready to close.

Some bands are ready for all five questions. Others may want to start with #1 and #5 or perhaps #1, #2, and #5.

The Closing

(Read in unison or by one member of the band)

Now to him who is able to do immeasurably more than all we ask or imagine, according to his power that is at work within us, to him be glory in the church and in Christ Jesus throughout all generations, for ever and ever! Amen.

(EPHESIANS 3:20–21)

TIME | TRUST – TRANSFORMATION

CHARACTERISTICS OF MOVEMENTS

Characteristics of a Renewal Movement

FROM *SIGNS OF THE SPIRIT: HOW GOD RESHAPES
THE CHURCH* BY HOWARD SNYDER

1. Thirst for renewal
2. Stress on the work of the Spirit
3. An institutional/charismatic tension
4. A concern for being a countercultural community
5. Nontraditional or non-ordained leadership
6. Ministry to the poor
7. Energy and dynamism

Six Characteristics of a Movement

FROM *MOVEMENTS THAT CHANGE THE WORLD: FIVE KEYS TO SPREADING THE GOSPEL* BY STEVE ADDISON

1. White-hot faith
2. Commitment to a cause
3. Contagious relationships
4. Rapid mobilization
5. Adaptive methods
6. Pioneering or apostolic leadership

Common Characteristics of Church Planting Movements

FROM *CHURCH PLANTING MOVEMENTS: HOW GOD IS REDEEMING A LOST WORLD* BY DAVID GARRISON

1. Extraordinary prayer
2. Abundant evangelism
3. Intentional planting of reproducing churches
4. The authority of God's Word
5. Local leadership
6. Lay leadership
7. House churches
8. Churches planting churches
9. Rapid reproduction
10. Healthy churches

10 Characteristics of Movemental Christianity

FROM *1,000 CHURCHES: HOW PAST MOVEMENTS DID IT—AND HOW YOUR CHURCH CAN, TOO* BY ED STETZER AND DANIEL IM

1. Prayer
2. Intentionality of multiplication
3. Sacrifice
4. Reproducibility
5. Theological integrity
6. Incarnational ministry
7. Empowerment of God's people
8. Charitability in appreciating other models
9. Scalability
10. Holistic overall approach

Roland Allen's Spontaneous Expansion of the Church

1. Begin with the teachings of Jesus
2. Give priority to evangelism
3. Follow a Pauline approach
4. Start indigenous (i.e., contextualized) churches
5. Trust in the work of the Spirit (and teach new believers to do the same)
6. Avoid devolution
7. Develop leaders from the new churches
8. Involve voluntary clergy and non-professional missionaries

FROM *ROLAND ALLEN: PIONEER OF SPONTANEOUS EXPANSION* BY J. D. PAYNE

MARKS OF A MOVEMENT ASSESSMENT TOOL

By Dr. Ed Love, Director of Church Multiplication, The Wesleyan Church

Throughout this book, Winfield Bevins has presented six marks of a movement from the Wesleyan revival of the eighteenth and nineteenth centuries. These marks are not theoretical ideals from days gone by—they are applicable for ministry today.

The following assessment tool was designed to help movement-minded leaders discover what ministry components are aligned with movement-centered thinking and what may need more attention. For better accuracy and team dialogue, consider involving other ministry leaders, board members, or key influencers by having each complete this assessment and compare the results.

Throughout the assessment, you will find a summary of each mark, followed by five evaluative questions. On a scale from 1–5 (five being the strongest value), circle the number representing your current context. Calculate the total for each mark at the bottom of the page. After you complete all six categories, calculate the overall total (out of 150 points) on the final page.

At the end of the assessment, a series of reflective coaching questions is available to help you clarify your next steps, both individually and organizationally.

6 Marks of a Movement

1. Changed lives
2. Contagious faith
3. The Holy Spirit
4. Disciple-making
5. Apostolic impulse
6. Organic multiplication

CHANGED LIVES

The life of John Wesley reminds us of the essential fact that movements are built on Christ, not people. When we look at the pages of church history, we see that multiplication movements happened through leaders who had a life-changing encounter with the living Christ. History is made by men and women of faith who have met the living God and cannot help but tell everyone they meet about the Good News of Jesus.

How often are people in your church invited into a life-transforming experience with Jesus Christ?

1	2	3	4	5
Never		Once in a while		All the time

Is it common for people in your church to publicly share about having a life-transforming encounter with Jesus Christ?

1	2	3	4	5
Never		Once in a while		All the time

Does the preaching and teaching ministry of your church help people understand the fullness of salvation through Christ alone?

1	2	3	4	5
No		Every now and then		Absolutely

When the leaders cast the vision for your church's ministry, do they place an emphasis on helping people far from God encounter Jesus Christ in a life-altering way?

1	2	3	4	5
Never		Once in a while		All the time

How many opportunities, outside of weekend worship gatherings, does your ministry create for people to encounter Jesus Christ in a meaningful way?

1	2	3	4	5
None	Bi-annually	Quarterly	Monthly	Weekly

Changed Lives Score _____/25

CONTAGIOUS FAITH

As a result of Wesley's decision to begin using lay ministers in the Wesleyan revival, people today have an open door to share in ministry in most churches. Lay leadership is one of the most common features of rapidly expanding church planting movements around the world. If we want to see a rapid multiplication movement today, it must be built on a model that empowers and releases all people for ministry and evangelism.

Does your church offer frequent training opportunities in evangelism?

1	2	3	4	5
Never		Once a year		Consistently

Does your church offer a spiritual gifts assessment or ministry mobilization course?

1	2	3	4	5
Never		Annually		Monthly

Does your church provide a clear pathway to get involved in the church's mission?

1	2	3	4	5
Not Really		Being developed		It's highly visible

Does your church provide or promote a basic church planting orientation course?

1	2	3	4	5
Annually		Quarterly		Monthly

Does your church have a reproducible format for training and networking future church planters?

1	2	3	4	5
No		Sort of		Yes

Contagious Faith Score _____/25

SPIRIT-EMPOWERED

The early church came alive and grew exponentially after the Holy Spirit came and while the first Jesus followers gathered together in prayer (see Acts 1:8). In the same way the church came to life on the day of Pentecost, the Wesleyan revival was founded upon the guiding influence of the Holy Spirit. As we look at other similar movements throughout history and even today, we find the Spirit's empowering work at the very core. It is impossible to understand multiplication movements without understanding the important role of the Spirit in the lives of the catalytic leaders.

How robust is your church's prayer culture?

1	2	3	4	5
Weak		Mediocre		Strong

How often does your church emphasize the person and work of the Holy Spirit in the church?

1	2	3	4	5
Never		Once in a while		All the time

Does your church have a consistent prayer/intercessory team in place?

1	2	3	4	5
No		A few people		Yes

How often does your church provide specific teaching/training on the role of the Holy Spirit?

1	2	3	4	5
As needs arise		Quarterly		Monthly

Does the Spirit's presence permeate the leadership culture and serving teams?

1	2	3	4	5
Not really		Occasionally		Absolutely

Spirit Empowered Score _____/25

DISCIPLESHIP SYSTEMS

In terms of Christian movements, the genius of Wesley was that he realized the importance of creating disciple-making systems. He organized people into three interlocking discipleship groups: societies, class meetings, and bands. Societies were larger gatherings of 50–70 people, providing worship and teaching (much like a new church). It was the smaller, more intentional class meetings (10–12 people) where deep discipleship happened. The bands (three to five people) were distinguished by high accountability.

What percentage of your church's weekend worship attendance are engaged in smaller groups for care, accountability, spiritual growth, and missional outreach?

1	2	3	4	5
0%	25%	50%	75%	100%

How would you describe the discipleship fervency throughout your church?

1	2	3	4	5
Low		Average		Very Strong

How does your church communicate lifestyle and spiritual growth expectations?

1	2	3	4	5
We don't		Verbally, when asked		Written down and regularly explained

Do your church's small group leaders view themselves as spiritual guides/disciple-makers?

1	2	3	4	5
Not really		Unknown		Absolutely

How would you describe the spiritual accountability environment in your church?

1	2	3	4	5
Nonexistent		Weak		Very strong

Discipleship Systems Score _____/25

APOSTOLIC LEADERSHIP

One cannot understand the Wesleyan revival without recognizing the apostolic nature of the movement. John Wesley was an apostolic leader who assimilated great men and women around him, allowing those individuals to become champions of the revival. Wesley was a strong leader with a God-given talent to recognize the best in people and develop leadership qualities in others.

Is the leadership in your church committed to discipling and developing future ministry leaders?

1	2	3	4	5
Not so much		Somewhat		Absolutely

Does the leadership in your church sense a burden to develop, empower, and send leaders (church starters) into other communities with the message of Jesus?

1	2	3	4	5
Not really		Somewhat		Obsessed

Does the pastoral leadership in your church have apprentices (potentially a future church planter)?

1	2	3	4	5
Not Yet		Undefined		Well-defined

How often does your church provide training or small group curriculum focused on developing future preachers, teachers, and communicators of biblical truth?

1	2	3	4	5
Annual event		Quarterly rallies		Weekly meetings

Does your church have an intentional means of evaluating the faithfulness and fruitfulness of your emerging leaders?

1	2	3	4	5
Nothing in place		Through conversations		Clearly defined process

Apostolic Leadership Score _____/25

6. ORGANIC MULTIPLICATION

The Wesleyan revival spread rapidly throughout the British Isles and North America. Methodism was a multiplication movement which reproduced everything: disciples, leaders, small groups, societies, and new churches. To keep up with the growth, the movement's leaders planted hundreds of new societies around the world. Societies were essentially faith communities planted in new geographic centers. These societies would quickly reproduce themselves by planting other societies in neighboring areas and surrounding towns to reach even more people with the message of Jesus.

How would you describe your church's desire to reproduce itself?

1	2	3	4	5
Low		Average		Strong

How does your church communicate the expectation for leaders to reproduce themselves?

1	2	3	4	5
We don't		Only when asked		Communicated everywhere

How does your church communicate the expectation that it will reproduce itself (as in planting a new expression of the church in another populace or people group)?

1	2	3	4	5
We don't		Only when asked		Communicated everywhere

Does your church measure and celebrate how many believers and leaders you are sending out to serve as pioneers of new faith communities?

1	2	3	4	5
No		Sort of		Absolutely

Does your church clearly understand your vision for rapid kingdom expansion through church multiplication?

1	2	3	4	5
Not really		I wish they did		They own it!

Organic Multiplication Score _____/25

Identifying Your Next Steps

1. Changed Lives   /25
2. Contagious Faith   /25
3. Spirit-Empowered   /25
4. Discipleship Systems   /25
5. Apostolic Leadership   /25
6. Organic Multiplication /25

Total   /150

Reflective Coaching Questions:

What 2–3 things can you celebrate in regard to the assessment?

How would you characterize the obstacles you are facing at this time?

What component will take you and your church more than a year to advance?

Who could you and your church learn from as you implement movement-minded changes?

What philosophical, theological, or practical questions are you wrestling with?

What are five practical things you could do in the next 45 days to begin implementing a movement-minded church culture?

If funding was not an obstacle, how would you address the issues facing your church planting movement?

ACKNOWLEDGMENTS

This book has been a labor of love over the last few years. It is the culmination of my own ministry journey and the influence of others upon my life and ministry. I would like to acknowledge several key people who have influenced me toward writing this book on the Wesleyan revival as a model for the recovery of a modern-day multiplication movement.

Although I am not a Methodist, I am especially grateful for the work of three of my heroes of the faith who are. The writings of Robert Coleman, Howard Snyder, and George Hunter III have greatly impacted my life and ministry over the years.

I am thankful for Steve Seamands, Jonathan Raymond, and Howard Snyder, who are in my weekly band meeting. We meet each week to pray for each other and ask deep questions about the state of our souls. I am profoundly grateful for this holy hour.

I am thankful for the New Room team, David Thomas, JD Walt, and Mark Benjamin for their passionate leadership and call for the church to sow for a Great Awakening. I have heard the call, and this book is my little contribution to the cause. I am honored to be a part of the team!

I am thankful for my friends Todd Wilson and Bill

Couchenour at Exponential, who are helping the church make and multiply disciples through church planting and church multiplication. I am excited to have this book in the Exponential book series.

Last but not least, I am so thankful for my editor at Zondervan, Ryan Pazdur, for his gracious spirit and his encouragement throughout the writing project. He is by far the best editor I have ever worked with. Thank you!

What we need in our day is a movement of disciple-making leaders who will lead movements that multiply disciples and churches in every city around the world. This book is dedicated to all the men and women around the world who are committed to disciple-making multiplication!

NOTES

INTRODUCTION

1. J. Wesley Bready, *England: Before and After Wesley* (New York: Russell & Russell, 1971), 19.
2. For a detailed discussion of England during Wesley's time period, Bready, *England: Before and After Wesley.*
3. John Wesley, *John Wesley's Sunday Service of the Methodist in North America* (United Methodist Publishing House, 1984), 10–11.
4. Albert Outler, *John Wesley* (Oxford: Oxford University Press, 1964), 335.
5. Thomas Jackson, *The Works of John Wesley* (Grand Rapids, MI: Baker Books, 1979, hereafter cited as *Works*), 13:146.
6. *Works*, 4:81.
7. See John H. Wigger, *Taking Heaven by Storm: Methodism and the Rise of Popular Christianity in America* (Urbana: University of Illinois Press, 1998); Roger Finke and Rodney Stark, *The Churching of America, 1776–2005: Winners and Losers in Our Religious Economy* (Piscataway, NJ: Rutgers University Press, 2005), 55ff.

8. George G. Hunter III, *The Recovery of a Contagious Methodist Movement* (Nashville, TN: Abingdon Press, 2011), 5.

9. See Howard Snyder, *The Radical Wesley*, (Franklin, TN: Seedbed Publishing, 2014), 5.

10. Ed Stetzer and Warren Bird, *Viral Churches: Helping Church Planters become Movement Makers* (San Fransisco, CA: Jossey Bass, 2010), 1.

11. Phil Zuckerman, *Living the Secular Life: New Answers to Old Questions* (New York: Penguin Books, 2015), 60.

12. For an in-depth study on the spirituality of youth and young adults, see Christian Smith and Melinda Lundquist Denton, *Soul Searching: The Religious Lives and Spiritual Lives of American Teenagers* (Oxford: Oxford University Press, 2005) and Christian Smith and Patricia Snell, *Souls in Transition: The Religious and Spiritual Lives of Emerging Adults* (Oxford: Oxford University Press, 2009). Their findings showed that the majority of youth adhere to a vague understanding of religion, which the authors call "Moralistic Therapeutic Deism" (or "MTD"). For statistics on the overall state of youth involvement in religion among North Americans, the Pew Research Center has observed that about one third of older Millennials—adults currently in their late 20s or early 30s—now say that they have no religion, which is up 9 percent among this age range from 2007. Nearly one quarter of Generation X now say that they have no particular religion, or they describe themselves as "atheists" or "agnostics". See http://www.pewforum.org/2015/05/12/americas-changing-religious-landscape/.

13. UK Census report on the state of relgion in Great Brittan. https://faithsurvey.co.uk/uk-christianity.html.

14. Leonard Sweet, *Postmodern Pilgrims* (Nashville, TN: B&H. 2000).

15. Sections from this book have been used with permission from the publisher out of Winfield Bevins, *Rediscovering John Wesley* (Cleveland, TN: Pathway Press, 2003).

CHAPTER 1

1. L. P. Gerlack and V. H. Hine, *People, Power, Change: Movements of Social Transformation* (New York: Bobbs-Merrill, 1970), 370–77.
2. George Hunter III, *The Recovery of a Contagious Methodist Movement* (Nashville, TN: Abingdon Press, 2011), 31–32.
3. Robert Coleman, *Master Plan of Evangelism* (Grand Rapids, MI: Revell, 1993), 27.
4. Rodney Stark, *The Rise of Christianity: A Sociologist Reconsiders History* (Princeton, NJ: Princeton University Press, 1996), 6–7.
5. Other books I would recommend to help you understand the movement dynamics of early Christianity are Roland Allen, *Missionary Methods: St Paul's Or Ours?* 4th ed. (London: World Dominion Press, 1912); Roland Allen, *The Spontaneous Expansion of the Church: And the Causes That Hinder it* (London: World Dominion Press, 1927); Paul Barnett, *The Birth of Christianity: The First Twenty Years* (Grand Rapids, MI: Eerdmans, 2005); Paul Barnett. *Paul: Missionary of Jesus* (Grand Rapids, MI: Eerdmans, 2008); Peter Bolt and Mark Thompson, *The Gospel to the Nations: Perspectives on Paul's Mission* (Downers Grove, IL: IVP Academic, 2001); Chris Green, *God's Power to Save: One Gospel for a Complex World?* (Leicester, U.K.: Inter-Varsity Press, 2006); I. Howard Marshall and David Peterson, *Witness to the Gospel: The Theology of Acts* (Grand Rapids, MI: Eerdmans, 1998); Paul E. Pierson, *The Dynamics of Christian Mission: History Through a Missiological Perspective* (Pasadena, CA: William Carey International University Press, 2008); Eckhard J. Schnabel, *Early Christian Mission: Jesus and the Twelve, Vol. I* (Downers Grove, IL: IVP Academic, 2004); Eckhard J. Schnabel, *Early Christian Mission: Paul and the Early Church, Vol. II* (Downers Grove, IL: IVP Academic, 2004); Eckhard J. Schnabel, *Paul the Missionary: Realities, Strategies and Methods* (Downers Grove, IL: IVP Academic, 2008); Ralph Winter, "The Two Structures of God's Redemptive Mission," *Perspectives on the World*

Christian Movement: A Reader (Pasadena, CA: William Carey Library Publishers, 1999); Ralph Winter and Steven Hawthorne, *Perspectives on the World Christian Movement: A Reader* (Milton Keynes, UK: Paternoster Press, 2009); Ralph D. Winter, *The Unfolding Drama of the Christian Movement* (Pasadena, CA: Institute of International Studies, 1979).

6. Rodney Stark, *The Rise of Christianity: A Sociologist Reconsiders History* (Princeton, NJ: Princeton University Press, 1996), 208.

7. Alan Kreider,. *The Patient Ferment of the Early Church. The Improbable Rise of Christianity in the Roman Empire* (Grand Rapids, MI: Baker Academic), 2016.

8. An important resource is Dale T. Irvin and Scott W. Sunquist, *History of the World Christian Movement: Volumes 1 and 2* (Maryknoll, NY: Orbis Books, 2001).

9. See Phillip Jenkins, *The Next Christendom: The Coming of Global Christianity* (New York: Oxford University Press, 2011).

10. For a quick overview of global Christianity see the report, "Status of Global Christianity, 2017, in the Context of 1900–2050" from the Center for the Study of Global Christianity at Gordon-Conwell Theological Seminary. http://www.gordonconwell.edu/ockenga/research/documents/StatusofGlobalChristianity2017.pdf

11. Pew Research Center, "Global Christianity: A Report on the Size and Distribution of the World's Christian Population." December 19, 2011, http://www.pewforum.org/2011/12/19/global-christianity-exec/

12. John Stott, *Christian Mission in the Modern World* (Downers Grove, IL: InterVarsity Press, 1975),

13. Martin Robinson, *Planting Mission-Shaped Churches Today* (Oxford, UK: Monarch Books, 2006), 144.

14. Timothy C. Tennent, "Homiletical Theology," Opening Convocation Address, Asbury Theological Seminary, September 2016, http://timothytennent.com/2016/09/13/my-2016-opening-convoca-tion-address-homiletical-theology/

15. Alvin L. Reid, *Radically Unchurched: Who They Are & How to Reach Them* (Grand Rapids, MI: Kregel Publications, 2002), 21.

16. George G. Hunter III, *The Recovery of a Contagious Methodist Movement* (Nashville, TN: Abingdon Press, 2011), 28.

17. Howard Snyder, *Signs of the Spirit: How God Reshapes the Church* (Eugene, OR: Wipf & Stock, 1997), 34. Other key books on Christian renewal movements include Jonathan Edwards, *A History of the Work of Redemption Containing the Outlines of a Body of Divinity* (Carlisle, PA: Banner of Truth Trust, 2003); Charles G. Finney, *Reflections on Revivals of Religion* (Virginia Beach, VA: CBN University Press, 1978); and more recent reflections by Richard F. Lovelace, *Dynamics of Spiritual Life: An Evangelical Theology of Renewal* (Downers Grove, IL: InterVarsity Press, 1979); William G. McLoughlin, *Revivals, Awakenings, and Reform* (Chicago: University of Chicago Press, 1978).

18. Ibid., 285–293.

19. George Hunter, *The Recovery of a Contagious Methodist Movement* (Nashville, TN: Abingdon Press, 2011). 10.

CHAPTER 2

1. Steve Addison, *Movements That Change the World: Five Keys to Spreading the Gospel* (Downers Grove, IL: InterVarsity Press, 2011), 37.

2. Elisha Coffman, "Attack of the Bible Moths" *Christian History Magazine*, Issue 69 (Vol. XX, No. 1), 20.

3. C.E. Vulliamy, *John Wesley*. (New York: Scribner, 1932), 55. Also cited in Howard Snyder, *The Radical Wesley*, 21.

4. For a detailed introduction on the Wesleys' failed mission to Savannah, see Geordan Hammond, *John Wesley in America: Restoring Primitive Christianity* (Oxford: Oxford Press, 2014). Hammond's book contributes to the debate on the importance of the Georgia mission for later developments in Methodism by providing a clear and detailed picture of the mission and its context.

5. *Works*, 1:23.

6. *Works*, 1:102.

7. Herbert McGonigle, *John Wesley and the Moravians* (England: The Wesley Fellowship, 1993), 24.

8. Thomas Jackson, *The Works of John Wesley* (Grand Rapids, MI: Baker Books, 1979), 1:103.

9. Albert Outler, *John Wesley* (New York: Oxford Press, 1964), 52.

10. Roland H. Bainton, *Here I Stand: A Life of Martin Luther* (Peabody, MA: Hendrickson Publishers, 1977), 48.

11. Dietrich Bonhoeffer, *The Cost of Discipleship* (New York: Touchstone, 1995), 89.

12. C. S. Lewis, *Mere Christianity* (New York: Collier Books, 1952), 72.

CHAPTER 3

1. Malcolm Gladwell, *The Tipping Point: How Little Things Can Make a Big Difference* (Boston: Little, Brown, 2000), 7.

2. Ibid., 26.

3. *Works*, 5:3.

4. John Gillies, ed. *Memoirs of the Reverend George Whitefield* (New Haven, CT: Whitmore and Buckingham and H. Mansfield, 1834), 28.

5. John Wesley, *The Works of John Wesley*, Vol. 19, Journal and Diaries II (1738–43), W. Reginal Ward and Richard P. Heitzenrater, eds. (Nashville, TN: Abingdon Press, 1990), 19:21.

6. *Works*, 1:185.

7. John Wesley, *The Works of John Wesley*, Vol. 26, The Letters II, Frank Baker, ed., (Nashville: Abingdon Press, 1987), 26:692.

8. *Works*, VIII: 317.

9. To find out more on Wesley's instructions to the early Methodist preachers see Richard P. Heitzenrater, *Wesley and the People Called Methodists*, 2nd ed. (Nashville, TN: Abingdon Press, 2013), 161.

10. Howard Snyder, *The Radical Wesley*, (Franklin, TN: Seedbed Publishing, 2014), 74–75.

11. Luke Tyerman, *Life and Times of the Rev. John Wesley* (New York: Harper and Brothers Publishers, 1872), 1:160–161

12. Gerald R. Cragg, *The Works of John Wesley,* Bicentennial ed. Vol. 11: *The Appeals to Men of Reason and Religion and Certain Open Letters* (Nashville, TN: Abingdon Press, 1975), 11:5.

13. Quoted in Douglas Bebb, *Wesley: A Man with a Concern* (London: Epworth, 1950),139.

14. Cragg, *The Works of John Wesley,* 29.

15. *Works,* 1:363.

16. Nehemiah Curnock, *The Journals of the Rev. John Wesley* (London: Epworth, 1938), 8:110.

17. Quoted in John Telford, *The Life of John Wesley* (London: Hodder & Stoughton, 1886), accessed through the Wesley Center for Applied Theology at Northwest Nazarene University, http://wesley.nnu.edu/john-wesley/the-life-of-john-wesley-by-john-telford/the-life-of-john-wesley-by-john-telford-chapter-14.

18. J. E. Hutton, *A History of the Moravian Church* (Fetter Lane, London: Moravian Publication Office, 1909), 207.

19. John Greenfield, *When the Spirit Came: The Story of the Moravian Revival of 1727* (Minneapolis, MN: Bethany Fellowship, 1967), 20.

20. Robert Coleman, *The Master Plan of Evangelism* (Grand Rapids, MI: Revell, 1972), 101.

21. D. Micheal Henderson, *John Wesley's Class Meeting: A Model for Making Disciples* (Nappanee, IN: Evangel Publishing House, 1997), 30.

22. Wesley actually had a discipleship ecosystem for small groups that included societies, class meetings, and bands. We will discuss them in a later chapter.

23. John Wesley, "Plain Account of the People Called Methodists," *The Works of John Wesley* Vol. 9, The Methodist Societies: History, Nature, and Design, Rupert Davies, ed. (Nashville, TN: Abingdon Press, 1989), 9:277.

24. Albert Outler, *John Wesley,* (Oxford: Oxford University Press, 1964), 86.

25. Ibid., 179.

26. Bready J. Wesley, *England: Before and After Wesley* (London: Hodder and Stoughton, n.d.) 238.

27. John Wesley, *Poetical Works,* I:IX-XXII; cited in D. Michael Henderson, *John Wesley's Class Meeting: A Model for Making Disciples* (Nappanee, IN: Evangel Publishing House, 1997), 86.

28. See John Finney, *Finding Faith Today: How Does it Happen?* (Swindon, UK: British and Foreign Bible Society, 1992), 46–47.

29. Ibid., 46.

30. Ibid., 47.

CHAPTER 4

1. For a deeper look at the work of the Holy Spirit in early Methodism, see two academic articles I have written on the important role of the Holy Spirit in John Wesley's theology: "Historical Development of Wesley's Doctrine of the Holy Spirit," *Wesleyan Theological Journal,* Fall 2006 and "Pneumatology in John Wesley's Theological Method," *The Asbury Theological Journal,* Vol. 58, No. 2, Fall 2003.

2. For a detailed overview of the topic, see Henry D. Rack, *Reasonable Enthusiast: John Wesley and the Rise of Methodism,* 3rd ed. (London: Epworth Press; 2014).

3. Paul Chilcote, *Recapturing the Wesleys' Vision.* (Downers Grove, IL: IVP Books, 2004), 55.

4. *Works,* 5:124, "The Witness of the Spirit."

5. *Works,* 5:124, "The Witness of the Spirit."

6. *Works,* "A Letter to a Roman Catholic."

7. *Works,* 10:79, "Letter to Rev. Dr. Middleton."

8. Howard Snyder, *The Radical Wesley,* (Franklin, TN: Seedbed Publishing, 2014), 157.

9. A. W. Tozer, *The Pursuit of God* (Camp Hill, PA: Christian Publications, 1993), 9.

10. *Works*, 8:340, "The Character of a Methodist."

11. *Works*, 5:3, "Preface."

12. *Works*, 14:220, "Abridgments of Various Works."

13. John Wesley, *Explanatory Notes Upon the New Testament*, (Salem, OH: Schmul Publishing Co., 2000), 554.

14. Telford, John, ed. *The Letters of the Rev. John Wesley*, 8 vols. (London: Epworth Press, 1931), 5:257.

15. *Works*, 5:38, "Scriptural Christianity."

16. Wesley attached the following footnote to the sermon: "It was not my design, when I wrote, ever to print the latter part of the following sermon: But false and scurrilous accounts of it which have been published, almost in every corner of the nation, constrain me to publish the whole, just as it was preached; that men of reason may judge for themselves" *Works*, 5:37.

17. John Telford, *The Life of John Wesley* (London: The Epworth Press, 1947), 394.

18. Steve Seamonds, "Pursuing Pentecost," *Good News Magazine*, Nov. 28, 2017, https://goodnewsmag.org/2017/11/pursuing -pentecost/

19. Randy Maddox, *Responsible Grace: John Wesley's Practical Theology* (Nashville, TN: Kingswood Books, 1994), 135.

20. Ted A. Campbell, *John Wesley and Christian Antiquity: Religious Vision and Cultural Change* (Nashville, TN: Kingswood Books, 1991), 83.

21. See Wayne Grudem and Stanley N. Gundry, eds., *Are Miracles for Today?* (Grand Rapids, MI: Zondervan, 1996) for a more in-depth discussion on the different views of spiritual gifts.

22. For a detailed introduction to the Pentecostal movement see Vinson Synan, *The Century of the Holy Spirit: 100 Years of Pentecostal and Charismatic Renewal* (Nashville, TN: Thomas Nelson Publishers, 2001), 1–12.

23. David Martyn Lloyd-Jones, *The Sovereign Spirit* (Wheaton, IL: Harold Shaw Publishers, 1985), 48.

CHAPTER 5

1. Leonard Sweet, *Aqua Church* (Loveland, CO: Group, 1999.), 8.

2. Howard Snyder, *The Radical Wesley*, (Franklin, TN: Seedbed Publishing, 2014), 54.

3. D. Michael Henderson, *John Wesley's Class Meeting* (Nappanee, IN: Evangel Publishing House, 1997), 69.

4. Malcolm Gladwell, *The Tipping Point. How Little Things Can Make a Big Difference* (New York: Little, Brown, 2000), 173.

5. *Works,* 3:144.

6. *Works,* 1:416.

7. Henderson, *John Wesley's Class Meeting: A Model for Making Disciples,* 112.

8. I will not be able to offer an in depth account of the historical development for the early Methodist structure because of lack of room in this short book, but would like to commend several important books that you might find helpful including Richard P. Heitzenrater, *Wesley and the People Called Methodists,* 2nd ed. (Nashville, TN: Abingdon, 2013); Kenneth J. Collins, *John Wesley: A Theological Journey,* (Nashville, TN: Abingdon, 2003); and Russell E. Richey, Kenneth E. Rowe, and Jean Miller Schmidt, *American Methodism: A Compact History* (Nashville, TN: Abingdon, 2012).

9. Albert C. Outler, *John Wesley* (Oxford: Oxford University Press, 1980), 178.

10. *Works,* 9:256–57.

11. Skevington Wood, *The Burning Heart, John Wesley: Evangelist.* (Minneapolis, MN: Bethany House, 1978), 191–192.

12. *Works,* VIII, 269–270.

13. George Hunter III, *To Spread the Power: Church Growth in the Wesleyan Spirit* (Nashville, TN: Abingdon Press, 1987), 56.

14. Henderson, *John Wesley's Class Meeting: A Model for Making Disciples,* 110.

15. Luke Tyerman, *Life and Times of the Rev. John Wesley* (New York: Harper and Brothers Publishers, 1872), 1:69–70.

16. Watson and Kisker, *The Band Meeting: Rediscovering Relational Discipleship in Transformational Community*, 77.
17. Albert C. Outler, *John Wesley* (Oxford: Oxford University Press, 1980), 181.
18. *Works*, 11:433.
19. Kevin Watson and Scott T. Kisker, *The Band Meeting: Rediscovering Relational Discipleship in Transformational Community* (Franklin, TN: Seedbed Publishing, 2017), 15.
20. Several books I would recommend about Celtic mission include George Hunter III, *The Celtic Way of Evangelism* (Nashville, TN: Abingdon, 2000); Thomas Cahill, *How the Irish Saved Civilization* (New York: Doubleday, 1995); Liam de Paor, *Saint Patrick's World: The Christian Culture of Ireland's Apostolic Age* (Dublin: Four Courts, 1993); Louis Gougaud, *Christianity in Celtic Lands: a History of the Churches of the Celtics* (London: Sheed and Ward, 1932); John Finney, *Recovering the Past: Celtic and Roman Mission* (London: Darton, Longman & Todd, 1996).
21. *Works*, 8:343.
22. John Wesley, *How to Pray: The Best of John Wesley on Prayer* (Uhrichsville, OH: Barbour Publishing, 2007), 52.
23. *Works*, 5:187. See also Henry H. Knight III, *The Presence of God in the Christian Life: John Wesley and the Means of Grace* (Metuchen, N.J.: Scarecrow Press, 1971).
24. *Works*, 5:187.
25. George Hunter III, *The Recovery of a Contagious Methodist Movement* (Nashville, TN: Abingdon Press, 2011), 15.
26. Robby Gallaty, *Rediscovering Discipleship: Making Jesus' Final Words Our First Work* (Grand Rapids, MI: Zondervan, 2017), 113.
27. John R. W. Stott, *"Make Disciples, Not Just Converts: Evangelism without Discipleship Dispenses Cheap Grace,"* Christianity Today, Vol. 43 No. 12 (October 25, 1999), 28.
28. Alan Hirsch, *The Forgotten Ways: Reactivating the Missional Church* (Grand Rapids, MI: Brazos Press, 2006), 45.

29. This conclusion is based upon two years of research Barna conducted regarding the current state of discipleship, and how churches might enhance the effectiveness of their discipleship ministries. See George Barna, *Growing True Disciples: New Strategies for Producing Genuine Followers of Christ* (Colorado Springs, CO: WaterBrook Press, 2001).

CHAPTER 6

1. Donald Thorson, *The Wesleyan Quadrilateral: Scripture, Tradition, Reason, and Experience as a Model of Evangelical Theology* (Grand Rapids, MI: Zondervan, 1990), 152.
2. *Works*, 7:423.
3. *Works*, 7:423.
4. *Works*, 5:38.
5. George Hunter III, cited in James C. Logan, ed. *Theology and Evangelism in the Wesleyan Heritage* (Nashville, TN: Kingswood Books, 1994), 159.
6. Alan Hirsch, *5Q: Reactivating the Original Intelligence and Capacity of the Body of Christ* (100 Movements, 2017), Xxxiii.
7. *Works*, 8:299.
8. *Works*, 5:3.
9. Maxwell Staniforth, ed. *Early Christian Writings: The Apostolic Fathers* (Middlesex, England: Penguin Classics, 1968), 85–92.
10. *Works*, 4:77.
11. John Wesley, Letter to Joseph Benson, Jan. 11, 1777, The Letters of John Wesley, Wesley Center Online, http://wesley.nnu.edu/john-wesley/the-letters-of-john-wesley/wesleys-letters-1777
12. David Garrison, *Church Planting Movements: How God Is Redeeming a Lost World* (Monument, CO: WIG Take Resources, 2004), 189.
13. John Wigger, *American Saint: Francis Asbury and the Methodists.* (Oxford: Oxford University Press, 2012), 3.
14. Telford, John, ed. *The Letters of the Rev. John Wesley,* Vol. 5 (London: Epworth Press, 1931), 257.

15. *Works*, 7:126.

16. There are many great books written on the role of women in ministry. However I would like to recommend *Relationshift: Changing the Conversation about Men and Women in the Church* by Sue Russell and Jackie Roese. The authors take a fresh look at the gender debate in the church. Rather than roles, the authors examine the Scriptural emphasis on relationships, specifically brother-sister type relationships based on love, humility, and mutuality. Instead of defining structured roles for men and women as argued by complementarian or egalitarian positions, this "relationarian" approach can be lived out in the existing structures of any culture. Focusing on relationships can enable the church to move beyond the divisions of the gender debate. See also Clouse, Bonnidell and Robert G., eds., *Women in Ministry: Four Views* (Downers Grove: IVP Books, 1989); and Beck, James R. and Blomberg, Craig L., eds., *Two Views on Women in Ministry* (Grand Rapids, MI: Zondervan, 2001).

17. Richard P. Heitzenrater, *Wesley and the People Called Methodists*, 2nd ed. (Nashville, TN: Abingdon Press, 2013), 160.

18. George Hunter III, *To Spread the Power: Church Growth in the Wesleyan Spirit* (Nashville: Abingdon Press, 1987), 62.

19. Steve Addison, *Movements That Change the World: Five Keys to Spreading the Gospel* (Downers Grove, IL: InterVarsity Press, 2011), 59.

20. Geoff Surratt, Greg Ligon, and Warren Bird, *The Multi-site Church Revolution* (Grand Rapids, MI: Zondervan, 2006), 161.

21. D. Michael Henderson, *John Wesley's Class Meeting: A Model for Making Disciples* (Nappanee, IN: Evangel Publishing House, 1997), 149.

22. Robert Coleman, *Nothing to Do but to Save Souls: John Wesley's Charge to His Preachers.* (Wilmore, KY: Wesley heritage Press, 1990), 21.

CHAPTER 7

1. *Works,* 5:39.
2. Richard Allen, *The Life Experience and Gospel Labors of the Rt. Rev. Richard Allen* (New York: Abingdon Press, reprint ed., 1960), 29–30.
3. There are a number of books and articles that discuss the theological connection between the Holiness movement and Pentecostalism. A few of them are: Donald Dayton, *Theological Roots of Pentecostalism* (New Jersey: Hendrickson Publishers, 1897); D. William Faupel, *The Everlasting Gospel: The Significance of Eschatology in the Development of Pentecostal Thought* (Sheffield, England: Sheffield Academic Press, 1996); Steve J. Land, *Pentecostal Spirituality: A Passion for the Kingdom* (Sheffield, England: Sheffield Academic Press, 1997); and Vinson Synan, *The Holiness-Pentecostal Tradition: Charismatic Movements in the Twentieth Century* (Grand Rapids, MI: Eerdmans , 1997).
4. *Works,* VIII: 299.
5. Telford, John, ed. *The Letters of the Rev. John Wesley,* Vol. 5 (London: Epworth Press, 1931), 257.
6. *Works,* 6:282–283.
7. *Works,* 6:309.
8. *Works,* 6:308.
9. *Works,* 6:311.
10. *Works,* 9:22.
11. David Hempton, *Methodism: Empire of the Spirit* (New Haven and London: Yale University Press, 2005), 2.
12. George Hunter III, *To Spread the Power: Church Growth in the Wesleyan Spirit* (Nashville: Abingdon Press, 1987), 56.
13. *Works,* 8:380–381.
14. *Works,* 10:138.
15. Howard Snyder, *The Radical Wesley,* (Franklin, TN: Seedbed Publishing, 2014), 64.
16. The information in this section is taken from David Garrison,

Church Planting Movements (Monument, CO: WIGTake Resources, LLC, 2004). See also David Watson, *Contagious Disciple Making: Leading Others on a Journey of Discovery* (Nashville, TN: Thomas Nelson, 2014); and Craig Ott and Gene Wilson, *Global Church Planting: Biblical Principles for Best practices for Multiplication* (Grand Rapids, MI: Baker Academic, 2011).

17. For my study of American Methodism, I have relied on several key resources including Roger Finke and Rodney Stark, *The Churching of America 1776–2005: Winners and Losers in Our Religious Economy*; Frank Baker, *From Wesley to Asbury: Studies in Early America Methodism* (Durham, NC: Duke University Press, 1976); John Wigger, *American Saint: Francis Asbury and the Methodists* (Oxford: Oxford University Press, 2009); and *Taking Heaven by Storm: Methodism and the Rise of Popular Christianity in America* (Urbana, IL: University of Illinois Press, 1998).

18. Roger Finke and Rodney Stark, *The Churching of America 1776–2005* (New Brunswick, NJ: Rutgers University Press, 2014), 68.

19. Quoted in Hallford E. Luccock and Paul Hutchinson, *The Story of Methodism* (Nashville, TN: Abingdon Press, 1926), 230.

20. Francis Asbury, *The Journal and Letters of Francis Asbury*, Vol. 3, Elmer T. Clark, ed. (Nashville, TN: Abingdon Press, 1958), 2:787.

21. John Wigger, *American Saint: Francis Asbury and the Methodists* (Oxford: Oxford University Press, 2009), 10.

CHAPTER 8

1. For two good books on the debate see Jerry L. Walls and Joseph R. Dongell, *Why I Am Not a Calvinist* (Downers Grove, IL: IVP Books, 2004); and Robert A. Peterson and Michael D. Williams, *Why I Am Not an Arminian* (Downers Grove, IL: IVP Books, 2004).

2. *Works,* 8:340.

3. *Works,* 8:347.

4. Roger E. Olson, "Don't Hate me because I'm Armenian," *Christianity Today,* Sept. 6, 1999.

5. C. S. Lewis, quoted in W. Vaus, *Mere Theology, A Guide to the Thought of C. S. Lewis* (Downers Grove, IL: InterVarsity Press, 2004), 167.

6. "Secularization" was first used to refer to the process of transferring property from ecclesiastical jurisdiction to that of the state or other non-ecclesiastical authority. In the institutional sense, "secularization" means the reduction of formal religious authority (e.g., in education). See D. W. Gill, "Secularism," *Evangelical Dictionary of Theology,* Walter A. Elwell ed., (Grand Rapids, MI: Baker Academic, 1984), 996.

7. W. C. Ringenberg, "Protestant Higher Education" *Dictionary of Christianity in America,* Daniel G. Ried, ed. (Downers Grove, IL: InterVarsity Press, 1990), 530.

8. Ibid., 530.

9. James Tunstead Burtchaell, *The Dying of the Light: The Disengagement of Colleges and Universities From Their Christian Churche.* (Grand Rapids, MI: Eerdmans, 1998). See also the works of Max Weber, *The Protestant Ethic and the Spirit of Capitalism* (New York: Scribner, 1958); *The Sociology of Religion* (Boston: Beacon Press, 1963).

10. John Wesley, *The Works of John Wesley* volumes (Grand Rapids, MI: Baker Books, 1991), 13:258.

11. Mark Liederbach and Alvin Reid, *The Convergent Church: Missional Worship in an Emerging Culture.* (Grand Rapids, MI: Kregel, 2009), 145.

12. Roger Finke and Rodney Stark, *The Churching of America, 1776–2005: Winners and Losers in Our Religious Economy* (Piscataway, NJ: Rutgers University Press, 2005), 160.

13. Ibid., 165.

14. William Warren Sweet, *Revivalism in America* (New York: Scribner, 1944), 163–164.
15. Ibid., 175.
16. Peter Cartwright, *Autobiography of Peter Cartwright, The Backwards Preacher*, W.P. Strickland, ed. (New York: Carlton and Porter, 1856), 523.
17. Richard Chartres, "New Fire in London," Lambeth Lecture, September 30, 2015, http://www.archbishopofcanterbury.org/articles.php/5621/bishop-of-london-delivers-lambeth-lecture-on-church-growth-in-the-capital.
18. This is taken from an online interview Ric Thorpe gave to Asbury Seminary. See it in full online at Asbury Seminary Voices, https://asburyseminary.edu/voices/26615.

CONCLUSION

1. *Works*, 8:346.
2. Francis A. Schaeffer, *Escape from Reason: A Penetrating Analysis of Trends in Modern Thought* (Downers Grove, IL: InterVarsity Press, 1968), 11–12.